The Atheist's Introduction to the New Testament

How the Bible Undermines the Basic Teachings of Christianity

Mike Davis

Outskirts Press, Inc.
Denver, Colorado

The opinions expressed in this manuscript are solely the opinions of the author and do not represent the opinions or thoughts of the publisher. The author represents and warrants that s/he either owns or has the legal right to publish all material in this book.

The Atheist's Introduction to the New Testament
How the Bible Undermines the Basic Teachings of Christianity
All Rights Reserved.
Copyright © 2008 Mike Davis
V2.0

This book may not be reproduced, transmitted, or stored in whole or in part by any means, including graphic, electronic, or mechanical without the express written consent of the publisher except in the case of brief quotations embodied in critical articles and reviews.

Outskirts Press, Inc.
http://www.outskirtspress.com

ISBN: 978-1-4327-2691-1

Outskirts Press and the "OP" logo are trademarks belonging to Outskirts Press, Inc.

PRINTED IN THE UNITED STATES OF AMERICA

CONTENTS

1. *Why This Book?* *1*
2. *Bible Basics and Translation Traps* *5*
3. *Rebutting the Rebuttals* *29*
4. *Contradictions in the Stories of Jesus's Birth* *45*
5. *Contradictions in the Crucifixion and Resurrection Stories* *67*
6. *Sin, Forgiveness and Salvation* *87*
7. *Jesus - God or Man?* *101*
8. *The End Was Near* *111*
9. *Paul Against Himself* *121*
10. *Phony Prophecies from the Old Testament* *138*
11. *Fighting Dirty - How to Use Ad Hominem Arguments Against Christian Hypocrites* *164*
12. *The Bottom Line* *179*

Chapter 1: Why This Book?

For me, Matthew 24:34 was the smoking gun. It proved to me that Christianity could not possibly be true. End of story. Case closed. It's the verse where Jesus tells his listeners that the judgment day will come before the generation he's speaking to passes away – meaning that some of them would still be alive when the sun went dark, the stars fell from the sky, and Jesus came riding down from heaven on clouds of glory. It's been nearly 2000 years now since that generation passed away, and the sun is still shining, the stars still twinkle in the sky, and clouds arrive with no passengers from heaven, glorious or otherwise. For me, this sealed the issue. Jesus was wrong. Therefore, he could not have been divine, but just a guy, preaching what he believed in, and no more deserving of our belief than any other guy.

It turned out that Matthew 24:34 was no fluke. As I read further in the Bible, I found other verses that basically said the same thing: Matthew 16:28, Mark 9:1 and 13:30, Luke 9:27 and 21:32. All say that the end would come while some of Jesus's original listeners were still alive. Again, all were wrong.

Even before discovering these verses I had been a non-believer for a number of years, but my unbelief was based primarily on the sheer silliness and implausibility of the Christian myth. If pressed, I could debate the average fundamentalist to a standoff, but was never able to deliver the knockout punch. When I started to study the New Testament seriously though, I found it to be filled with more contradictions and inconsistencies than I ever imagined or remembered from my days in Baptist Sunday School. It's been said that you can use the Bible to prove anything. It turns out that you can use the Bible to prove that the Bible itself is untrustworthy. If you are familiar with these biblical flaws, you can easily prevail in any debate with the typical Christian fundamentalist. But chances are if you're an atheist, agnostic, skeptic, or doubter you don't have either the time or the inclination to dive deeply enough into the Bible on your own to uncover the logical and historical flaws it contains. That's where this book comes in. It gives you the verbal ammunition you need to forcefully and convincingly refute the views of those Christians who believe the Bible to be the unerring word of God. After reading this book, the next time you see well-dressed young Christian missionaries coming up to your door, you will welcome them as the wolf welcomes the lamb, instead of hiding behind the front door until they go away.

But it's not just the personal satisfaction of scoring debate points that drives me to write this book. Although it may appear that most people have already made up their minds about such matters, the truth is that there are many individuals who aren't sure what to think about the Bible and Christianity. Some lean toward skepticism, others are still tilting toward Christianity. Many are plagued by doubt about Christian teachings, but fear the consequences of being wrong if the stories of sin and hellfire turn out to be true. Perhaps you yourself are a wavering believer just now testing the waters of skepticism, but fearful of turning loose completely and letting reason and logic lead you to the truth. If this is you, you can relax. You are not going to hell. This book shows you why. It turns out that the basic writings of the Christian religion are so full of absurdity, contradiction and discord that the only way to maintain the truth of Christian doctrine is to ignore the Bible itself. Fortunately for most Christian churches, this is not a problem, because most Christians do not read the Bible seriously, and are woefully unaware of its contents, except for what their preachers tell them on Sunday mornings.

Finally, this volume is not just an attack on Christianity, but an attack on irrationality. Prejudice against reason and logic is widespread in today's world, and in the United States especially an anti-intellectual bias is deeply rooted. Thanks to their disproportionate political influence, the Christian right have succeeded in dominating the political vocabulary to such an extent that science is now seen as just another special interest group, and no political candidate can afford to be viewed as lacking in "faith," which is the new euphemism for "religion." From stem cell research to global warming and the teaching of evolution, many of our political leaders are afraid to follow where the scientific evidence leads for fear of alienating that portion of the electorate that believes Jesus will soon return, perhaps even today or tomorrow. Maybe, just maybe, by dragging the inconsistencies of their religious dogmas into the light of day, we can begin to discredit the religionists, and chip away at the prestige and influence that these short-sighted anti-humanists have on the direction of our society as a whole. It may work. At least it's worth a try.

In William Golding's novel *Lord of the Flies*, Piggy is asked if he believes there are ghosts. He replies, "Course there aren't . . . 'Cos things wouldn't make sense. Houses an' streets, an' TV - they wouldn't work." The insightful Piggy realized that the irrational is incompatible with our natural striving to make the world more hospitable in relation to human needs and aspirations. There is a natural order to the world. By using our intelligence to understand that order and make it work for us, we can improve the lot of real human beings for the time that we all share this earth. But if irrationality wins, humankind loses. Belief in Christianity requires people to ignore their intelligence, suspend logic, strangle their reason. There are many fronts on which to fight against irrationality, and we have to pick our battles. This is mine.

Chapter 2: Bible Basics and Translation Traps

First, let's cover some background material that will help provide context for our discussions on biblical contradictions. Based on recent surveys[1] that reveal an astounding lack of religious knowledge among Americans – even among those who claim to be religious themselves – when you finish this chapter, you'll know more about the Bible than most Christians do.

What Is The Bible?

When you see it on the shelves at the bookstore, the Christian Bible appears to be a single book. In fact it is a collection of many books, 66 in all[2], by many authors, written over a period of hundreds of years. With few exceptions, the authors of these books are anonymous. There are many types of writing in the Bible. Some of it appears to be historical, although the authors did not adhere to the same standards of scholarship that modern historians hold. There are also poems, hymns, folk tales, instructions on how to live one's life, and warnings of impending doom. There are two main divisions, known to Christians as the

---

[1] Susan Jacoby, "Blind Faith," *Washington Post,* March 4, 2007. Review of Stephen Prothero's *Religious Literacy.*
[2] Even this statement requires qualification. Some Christian Bibles contain additional books, known collectively as *apocrypha,* some of which have at various times been considered authoritative by certain groups of Christians, including the Roman Catholic Church.

Old Testament (39 books) and the New Testament (27 books). The Old Testament contains the ancient Jewish scriptures, and the New Testament contains additional books that serve as the foundation of Christianity. Jews object to the term "Old Testament" as implying that their scriptures are somehow out of date, and they simply refer to the Old Testament as "the Bible." Jews do not recognize the New Testament as being sacred or having any religious authority whatsoever. Christians claim to consider both Old and New Testament as sacred scripture, but most practicing Christians do not give a lot of attention to the Old Testament except for the "prophecies" it supposedly contains with respect to the coming of Jesus. Jews, who take the Old Testament rather seriously, do not find any such prophecies in it, and go to great lengths to refute such claims. Additionally, the creation stories in Genesis receive some attention whenever the fundamentalists feel threatened by the teaching of evolution in the public schools. There is much savagery in the Old Testament, such as when Joshua's armies massacred all the inhabitants of Jericho and Ai (on God's orders), but Christians prefer not to call attention to the moral implications of such stories. Indeed, most Christians have only a passing familiarity with the Bible, and rarely study it seriously.

The New Testament describes the life of Jesus and the beginnings of the theological enterprise which turned him into the god Jesus Christ and established the orthodox Christian churches. Jesus, we are told, was an itinerant healer and preacher who lived and preached in the area of modern day Israel and what is now the Palestinian west bank region. During Jesus's time, the lands in this region were under either the direct or indirect control of the Roman Empire. Some of his followers, and perhaps Jesus himself, considered him to be the Jewish messiah, a long-awaited military leader who would rally the Jewish nation and lead it to glorious victory over the oppressors from Rome. But instead of leading Israel to triumph, Jesus was captured by the Roman authorities and executed by being nailed to a cross, a brutal form of execution known as crucifixion. After his crucifixion, some of his followers put a different interpretation on his death, and put out the story that Jesus had risen from the dead, and that his death was actually a sacrifice to atone for all the sins of mankind. According to this view, anyone who believed that Jesus died and was raised again would be saved from the consequences of his or her own sin. Those who did not believe would be tormented forever in hell as punishment for their transgressions against God's commandments. As we shall see later, even this basic message is not consistently reflected in the biblical text, but is contradicted repeatedly in the New Testament writings themselves.

The books of the New Testament can be categorized by type. There are four gospels which portray the life of Jesus. Tradition has it that two of the gospel authors, Matthew and John, were among Jesus's original twelve disciples, while the other two gospels (Mark and Luke) were written by men who traveled around with Peter and Paul respectively. Modern scholars discount this tradition of authorship on various grounds relating to the internal content of the books themselves, and thus consider the authorship of all four gospels to be anonymous. However, it is generally agreed that whoever wrote the gospel of Luke also wrote the book of Acts, which covers the activities of Peter and Paul in the years immediately after the death of Jesus. In spite of this scholarly opinion as to anonymous authorship, all four gospels continue to be known by their traditional names, and we will refer to them in that way as well. Thus when we say "Matthew says . . ." this is understood as shorthand for "the anonymous author of the gospel traditionally attributed to Matthew says . . ."

There are also a number of epistles (letters) in the New Testament, written to the early Christian congregations on various matters of doctrine. Several of these letters were written by Paul himself, who originally was a persecutor of the early Christians, but later became an ardent spokesman for the Jesus movement. Some scholars credit Paul with being the true founder of Christianity as a separate religion, as distinct from a mere Jewish sect, because Paul was primarily responsible for bringing the message of Jesus's death and resurrection to non-Jewish populations. The letters generally accepted by scholars to be authentic letters of Paul are (in chronological order of composition): 1st Thessalonians, 1st Corinthians, Philippians, Philemon, Galatians, 2nd Corinthians, and Romans. This attribution is based primarily on internal analysis of the letters themselves, comparison of vocabulary and style, and internal historical references. These genuine letters of Paul are the earliest Christian writings, having been written some decades before the gospels.

The New Testament includes other letters that were traditionally attributed to Paul, but which are now the subject of debate among scholars as to whether Paul was the true author.[3] He may have written them, but there is presently no consensus among the experts who study such things. This group of letters includes Ephesians, Colossians, and 2nd Thessalonians.

---

[3] L. Michael White, *From Jesus to Christianity* (Harper Collins, 2004), p.146.

A third category contains New Testament letters which were traditionally attributed to prominent early followers of Jesus – including Paul – but are now also considered by modern scholars to be of unknown authorship. This group includes the letters 1st and 2nd Timothy, Titus, Hebrews, James, 1st and 2nd Peter, 1st, 2nd, and 3rd John, and Jude.

Finally, there is the book of Revelation, a fantastic portrayal of the violently destructive end times when Jesus will come riding in on a cloud of glory to judge the living and the dead, assisted by various hideous monsters who are vividly described. "Revelation" is the English translation of the Greek word "apocalypse." The Book of Revelation is either highly symbolic, or highly confusing, or both, and there is no consensus even among scholars or Christians as to what its author is really trying to tell us.

Who's Who In The New Testament

If you didn't grow up in a religious family or attend Sunday school as a child, you might not be familiar with the cast of characters we'll encounter in studying the New Testament. To help set the stage, here's a brief introduction to some of the names we'll run across as we examine the contradictions of the New Testament:

Jesus of Nazareth

A traveling Jewish preacher and faith healer from the village of Nazareth in the region of Galilee, located in the northern portion of what is now Israel. He taught people to repent of their sins and to live a holy life in order to prepare for the kingdom of God. Many of his followers (and perhaps Jesus himself) considered him to be the

Jewish messiah, who would restore Israel's ancient independence and glory by rising up against the Roman Empire, which ruled the lands of the Middle East during Jesus's lifetime. Most biblical scholars assume that Jesus actually existed, but there is no historical evidence from his lifetime that would corroborate this. He did not leave any writings, and he is not mentioned in the writings of others who lived at the same time – at least not any that have survived to the present day. The first written references to him occur several decades after he is supposed to have died.

Christ (or Jesus Christ)

The primary god of the Christian religion. Christians call him the Son of God, but also say that he existed in the beginning with God the Father, and is of the same essence as God and of equal stature. Orthodox Christian doctrine teaches that because of mankind's sinfulness Christ came to earth in the person of Jesus and was crucified as a sacrifice for the sins of man. Those who believe in and accept his sacrifice are saved from the consequences of their sin and will spend eternity in heaven. Those who do not believe are condemned to eternal punishment in the fires of hell. The word Christ is from the Greek *christos*, which is itself a translation of the Hebrew *messiah*, meaning the anointed one. The Hebrew term was used of the Jewish kings in the Old Testament, and as we have seen, eventually came to signify Israel's future liberator. Christians further modified the meaning of the word to refer to the sacrificial son of God who atones for the sins of the world. In the mind of the average Christian, there is often not a clear distinction between Jesus the man and Christ the god, and the two are often confounded.

God

In the Old Testament, "God" was Yahweh, the Hebrew tribal god, translated as "LORD" (all capitals) in most English translations of the Bible. He was the creator of all that existed. Yahweh was a forceful personality, often becoming personally involved in the affairs of the Jews, his chosen people. In the New Testament, Yahweh is not mentioned by name, but "God" has become a more remote figure, less involved in the worldly affairs of mankind. Jesus often refers to God as "the Father" or "my Father." The Christian doctrine of the Trinity considers God the Father to be of the same divine essence as Christ and the Holy Spirit.

Holy Sprit

The third and most mysterious member of the Christian Trinity. The Holy Spirit (or Holy Ghost) is only vaguely described in the New Testament. However, it plays a significant role as the impregnator of Mary, the mother of Jesus. In many contexts, the "Holy Spirit" seems almost indistinguishable from God himself.

Son of Man

In the gospels, a phrase used by Jesus to refer to himself. When it appears in the Old Testament it generally refers to "man" as distinct from God, but the book of Daniel uses it apocalyptically, referring to the Son of Man arriving on clouds from heaven. It is this latter sense in which Jesus uses the term in the gospels.

Satan (the Devil)

The adversary of God and of Christ. In the Old Testament, God (Yahweh) was the source of all things good and evil, and Satan was simply a member of God's heavenly court.[4] But by the time of Jesus, God came to be seen as only the author of good things,[5] and Satan became his adversary and the source of all evil. This adversarial view, which sees the world as a battleground for competing forces of good and evil, is expressed in this passage from 1st John: "For this purpose the Son of God was manifested, that he might destroy the works of the devil." (1 John 3:8) In Revelation 12:7-9 Satan and his angelic troops are eventually defeated by God's angels under the command of the archangel Michael.

Paul

Originally known as Saul, he persecuted the early followers of Jesus, until he had a vision of Christ on the way to Damascus, after which he was converted to the new religion and became one of its most energetic spokesmen. He is the author of several letters in the New Testament, written to early Christian churches to encourage them in their belief and to correct their theological errors.

---

[4] *The New Oxford Annotated Bible.* (Oxford University Press, 1973), p.1150 (note to Zechariah 3:1). The name "Satan" means "adversary."

[5] Ibid., p.518 (note to 1 Chronicles 21:1).

Paul was primarily responsible for spreading the story of Christ to non-Jews, and some scholars credit him with being the true founder of Christianity as a non-Jewish religion centered on Christ the Savior, as opposed to a Jewish sect centered on Jesus as the Jewish messiah.

Pontius Pilate

Governor of the Roman province of Judea, which included Jerusalem. He held this office from 26 AD to 36 AD. According to the gospels, he presided over the trial of Jesus and sentenced him to death by crucifixion.

The Twelve Disciples

A select group of Jesus's followers, chosen by him to help heal the sick, cast out demons, and spread the word about the kingdom of God. They are Simon (Peter), his brother Andrew, James and John the sons of Zebedee, Philip, Bartholomew, Thomas, Matthew, James the son of Alphaeus, Simon the Zealot, Judas Iscariot, and finally either Thaddaeus or Judas son of James, or perhaps Nathanael, depending on which gospel you're reading. In the New Testament, Peter has the most prominent role of the twelve, followed by Judas Iscariot as the one who betrayed Jesus to the Romans. The others play very small parts, and some, such as Bartholomew and Thaddaeus, are only mentioned in the list of disciples' names, but do not appear again.

John the Baptist

A traveling Jewish preacher who was active before Jesus began his ministry. John taught that people should repent of their sins and be baptized, and the gospels tell us that John "prepared the way" for Jesus himself. (He is not to be confused with John of the twelve disciples, or John the traditional author of several New Testament books.)

Joseph

Husband of Mary, and the earthly father of Jesus, according to the gospels of Matthew and Luke.

Mary

Mother of Jesus and wife of Joseph. According to the gospels of Matthew and Luke, she gave birth to Jesus while still a virgin, having been impregnated by the Holy Spirit.

Pharisees

A Jewish religious sect who met together and studied the Jewish law and scriptures under the guidance of a teacher. Contrary to their portrayal in the gospels as strict legalists, the Pharisees took a fairly tolerant view of the Law, and were concerned with how the requirements of the Law could be reconciled with the demands of everyday life. In the gospels, Jesus is often portrayed as debating points of law with the Pharisees.

Sadducees

A Jewish religious sect closely aligned with the high priests and officials of the Temple. Their view of the Law was stricter and more conservative than that of the Pharisees. They are thought to have collaborated with the Roman occupiers of Jerusalem, which may account for the dominant position they held with respect to other Jewish groups.

Establishment Of The Christian Churches

It would be misleading and incorrect to speak of "the Church" in the context of the earliest Christian communities. The first Christian "churches" were nothing more than groups of believers meeting in the house of one of their members. In fact, the Greek word *ekkleisia*, which is usually translated as "church" in English, has as its core meaning "assembly" or "congregation." The book of Acts describes some of the activities and doctrinal disputes of this early period. Also, Paul's letters were written to some of these first congregations, in an attempt to return them to the correct path after they had been led astray by various forms of what Paul considered heretical teaching.

For about 250 years, the Christian movement was a minority sect within the Roman Empire, occasionally tolerated, occasionally persecuted, but having no official status. In the year 313, the emperor Constantine decreed in the Edict of Milan that all forms of worship, including Christianity, would be tolerated throughout the empire. Christians often assert that Constantine's edict made Christianity the "official" religion of the empire but this is claiming too much. The emperor's decree was in fact a statute of religious toleration, as we can see from this excerpt: "No one whatsoever should be denied freedom to devote himself either to the cult of the Christians or to such religion as he deems best suited for himself."[6] For several

---

[6] Quoted in Charles Freeman, *The Closing of the Western Mind* (Vintage, 2005), p.159.

centuries after the Edict of Milan, the Church was still dominated by the personalities of individual bishops, and during this time, the bishop of Rome, who eventually achieved the status of pope, was no more influential than others, and was actually less influential than bishops in some of the empire's great eastern cities such as Alexandria. During this period, some of the doctrines that we now associate with Christian orthodoxy, such as the Trinity and the divinity of Jesus, were hotly debated, with theological positions being declared now orthodox, now heretical, until one faction eventually became dominant within the Church, and forever after defined what it meant to be an orthodox Christian.[7]

In the eleventh century, due partly to theological disputes, but primarily because of increasing political, cultural, and linguistic differences, the eastern portion of the Church split away and became the eastern (or Greek) Orthodox Church, as distinct from the western (Roman) Catholic Church. ("Catholic" in Greek means "universal.") Later, in the 16th century, Martin Luther and others challenged the authority of the Catholic Church in Europe, and led a movement to reestablish what they viewed as a purer form of Christianity, relying less on the church and its priesthood as intermediaries between God and the individual believer, and more on direct access to God and the Bible by the common people. This movement is known as the Protestant reformation. The reformation did not directly establish a new church as such, but the ideas behind the reformation led to the founding of a number of Protestant Christian denominations such as the Baptists,

---

[7] A very readable account of these early doctrinal debates is found in Bart D. Ehrman, *Lost Christianities* (Oxford University Press, 2003)

Methodists, Lutherans, Presbyterians, and numerous smaller groups. None of these recognize the authority of the Roman Catholic Church in matters of doctrine or anything else. Minor doctrinal disputes distinguish the various Protestant denominations from each other, but these differences are of little interest to the outsider.

The Languages of the Bible

No part of the Bible was written in English. This may seem obvious, but it's a fact that sometimes gets lost in the heat of debate. The Old Testament books were all written in Hebrew, while the New Testament was composed entirely in Greek. This is a result of the different time periods in which the books were written. The conquests of Alexander the Great in the 4th century BC spread Greek language and culture throughout the Mediterranean area, including the Middle East. At the time during which Jesus lived and died, Greek was the common language spoken in government and business circles throughout the area. Many of the common people spoke Aramaic, which was a Semitic language related to Hebrew and to modern Arabic. But a good many of them probably spoke Greek as well. It's generally thought that Jesus's native language was Aramaic. It is not certain whether he also spoke Greek. Not long before Jesus's time, knowledge of the Hebrew language had declined to the point where even the Jews had their scriptures translated from Hebrew into Greek. This translation was known as the Septuagint, or the LXX, after the seventy scholars who, according to legend, worked on the translation. It is the oldest version of the Jewish scriptures now extant, older than any of the existing Hebrew texts.

Just as the books of the Bible were not originally written in English, they also were not originally divided into verses. It was many centuries after their composition before "chapter and verse" could be cited from the books of the Bible. This innovation is credited to Robert Estienne (aka Stephanus), who in 1551 published an edition of the Greek New Testament divided into verses.[8]

Before the reformation, the Bible in Europe existed almost exclusively in Latin translation. Since most common people could not read Latin, this presented a barrier to the average churchgoer, who had to rely on Church officials to explain what the Bible said and meant. The rise of Protestantism stimulated a number of projects to translate the Bible into the modern European languages spoken by ordinary people. Not everyone viewed this as a positive development, especially the Catholic hierarchy, which remained powerful. Translation of the Bible into the vernacular was considered heretical by the established church, and those who undertook it risked their lives in doing so. William Tyndale, to whom we owe much of the wording of the King James translation, was burned at the stake in 1536 on a charge of heresy for translating the Bible into English. (If you look at a copy of his New Testament translation, you will see that it has chapters, but no verses, as it was published before Stephanus added the verse divisions with which we are now familiar.)

It is important to realize that no "original" exists for the Bible, either for the Old or New Testament. We have copies

---

[8] Bart D. Ehrman, *Misquoting Jesus.* (Harper Collins, 2005), p. 80.

Bible Basics and Translation Traps

of numerous ancient manuscripts, over a period of some centuries, of varying completeness and quality, which scholars have studied and compared, in order to come up with their best judgment of what the original texts must have looked like. There are discrepancies and disagreements even with respect to these ancient manuscripts, and for uncertain passages, most Bible editions will give alternative manuscript readings in the footnotes. This variety of textual sources is a source of discomfort for many Christian apologists who have difficulty accepting that the "unerring word of God" is plagued by so many uncertainties.

Throughout the English-speaking world, those readers who do not know Greek or Hebrew must rely on English translations to tell them what the biblical authors said. There are many such translations, as you can see by visiting any large bookstore. They generally fall on a continuum from literal translation to paraphrase. Sometimes these endpoints on the continuum are referred to as "what the author said" and "what the author meant." To go into this topic in any detail would take us too far from our intended purpose, but the general point to keep in mind is that some Bible translations give you, as nearly as possible, the English equivalent of the Greek written by the New Testament authors. Other translations operate on the premise that the literal words are sometimes confusing and misleading, or subject to theological misinterpretation, due to differences in culture and environment, so they amend the literal translation to fit a modern context and/or the translator's theological understanding of the text. Moving further along the continuum, still other versions are not translations at all, but paraphrases of the biblical text. The premise underlying these paraphrases is that ordinary readers are so lacking in their knowledge of English, that they will be unable to grasp

19

the meaning of a true translation. So the paraphraser will tell the story in simpler language that conveys the gist of what the author said, but not the literal message. Paraphrases are not recommended for serious study. Unless you can read Greek, you are better off using one of the more literal English translations. This reduces the chance that you may take a translator's interpretation for the actual wording of the Bible itself.

A good choice from the literal end of the spectrum is the Revised Standard Version (RSV). The King James Version (KJV) is also an excellent choice from the literal end of the spectrum, but its translators relied on a relatively late Greek manuscript text and so the KJV does not have the advantage of being based on the more ancient Greek manuscripts that have come to light since 1611. Some readers find the obsolete English of the KJV to be intimidating, but it is easier than reading Shakespeare, so if you have some prior acquaintance with 17th century English literature, you will not find the language of the KJV to be a problem. However, readers need to be aware that some English words have undergone a change in meaning during the 400 years since the KJV was published, so caution is advised, in order to avoid misinterpretation.

The New American Standard Bible (NASB) is by and large a very literal translation, although as we'll see from the examples below, there are occasional passages where its translation becomes somewhat creative. The New International Version (NIV) is slightly less literal, but is in very readable English, and is the current best seller among Bible translations. The NIV is the product of more conservative scholars and unfortunately tends to obscure some of the contradictions and difficulties in the biblical text by hiding them under a translation that eliminates the contradiction. Finally, some versions of the Bible are rendered so freely into contemporary English that the literal meaning is thoroughly obscured. They are not recommended for anyone whose purpose is to study what the Bible actually says. Examples include The Living Bible or The Message.

Translation Traps

Sometimes translations express the theological agenda of the translators. Passages that are theologically embarrassing may be modified in the translation, or contradictions may be covered up. To give you a feel for how the meaning of a passage can be altered depending on which translation you're reading, let's look at a verse from Luke. In this passage, Luke 22:70, Jesus is being questioned before the Jewish council (i.e., the Sanhedrin) about claims that he is the son of God. How did Jesus answer this question? That depends on which translation you select.

Literal translation of the Greek:

> And they all said, are you then the son of God?
> And he said to them, **You say that I am.**

And here's how it's translated in several well-known English versions:

Revised Standard Version (RSV):

> And they all said, "Are you the Son of God, then?" And he said to them, "**You say that I am.**"

King James Version (KJV):

> Then said they all, Art thou then the Son of God? And he said unto them, **Ye say that I am.**

New American Standard Bible (NASB):

> And they all said, "Are You the Son of God, then?" And He said to them, "**Yes, I am.**"

New International Version (NIV):

> "They all asked, "Are you then the Son of God?" He replied, "**You are right in saying I am.**"

Contemporary English Version (CEV):

> Then they asked, "Are you the Son of God?" Jesus answered, "**You say I am!**"

> (Note the exclamation point. The CEV also has a footnote giving the alternative rendering "That's what you say.")

The Message:

> They all said, "So you admit your claim to be the Son of God?" "**You're the ones who keep saying it,**" he said.

New Living Translation (NLT):

> They all shouted, "So, are you claiming to be the Son of God?" And he replied, "**You say that I am.**"

As you can see, even in this simple verse, there is considerable variety in the renderings, and some of these differences have theological implications. Did Jesus call himself the son of God or not? Not in the original, but depending on the translation that you use, you might get the impression that he did. Note also how the question from the Sanhedrin, "Are you then the son of God?" takes on a more dramatic and confrontational tone by changing "they all said" to "they all shouted" in the NLT, or "So you admit your claim to be the Son of God?" in the Message. The RSV and KJV are the closest to the original. NASB, which is usually very literal, departs from the original in this particular verse.

What we learn from this is that some contradictions in the original may be obscured by the translation, to the extent that the unsuspecting reader would not even notice that a contradiction exists. A good example of this would be the differing accounts of Paul's conversion experience on the road to Damascus. These occur in Acts 9:7 and Acts 22:9. This is a well-known contradiction, which has received considerable attention from the apologists as they attempt to explain away the straightforward meaning of the conflicting passages.

Although he was originally a persecutor of the early Christian movement, Saul of Tarsus (later known as Paul), is reported to have experienced a conversion while traveling on the road to Damascus. As described in Acts 9, there was a sudden flash of light which knocked Saul to the ground, and a voice from the sky asking, "Saul, Saul, why are you persecuting me?" Saul was temporarily blinded by the flash, and was led into Damascus by his fellow travelers. In Damascus, his sight was restored, and Saul began to preach Jesus as the son of God and the means of salvation.

This story is told three times in the book of Acts: Acts 9:1-21; Acts 22:6-16; and Acts 26:12-20.

The first version is told in the third person, while in the second and third versions the character of Paul speaks for himself. But there is an inconsistency between the first two versions as to whether the men traveling with Saul also heard the voice from the sky. Acts 9:7 says that Paul's traveling companions heard the voice that Paul heard, but Acts 22:9 tells us that they did not.

Here are the two verses juxtaposed, first in a literal translation of the Greek, and then in several English translations. Notice how the contradiction inherent in these verses disappears in some of the translations:

Literal translation of the Greek:

> (Acts 9:7) Now the men journeying with him stood speechless, **hearing indeed the voice** but seeing no one.

> (Acts 22:9) Now those being with me indeed saw the light, but **they did not hear the voice** of the one speaking to me.

Revised Standard Version (RSV):

> (Acts 9:7) The men who were traveling with him stood speechless, **hearing the voice** but seeing no one.

> (Acts 22:9) Now those who were with me saw the light but **did not hear the voice** of the one who was speaking to me.

King James Version (KJV):

> (Acts 9:7) And the men which journeyed with him stood speechless, **hearing a voice**, but seeing no man.

Bible Basics and Translation Traps

> (Acts 22:9) And they that were with me saw indeed the light, and were afraid, but **they heard not the voice** of him that spake to me.

New American Standard Bible (NASB):

> (Acts 9:7) The men who traveled with him stood speechless, **hearing the voice** but seeing no one.

> (Acts 22:9) And those who were with me saw the light, to be sure, but **did not understand the voice** of the One who was speaking to me.

New International Version (NIV) and Today's New International Version (TNIV):

> (Acts 9:7) The men traveling with Saul stood there speechless; **they heard the sound** but did not see anyone.

> (Acts 22:9) My companions saw the light, but **they did not understand the voice** of him who was speaking to me.

In this case, the contradiction is there in the original, and in the translations that give the most literal rendering (RSV, KJV). But the other translations cover it up by adding a distinction between "hearing" the voice and "understanding" the voice, or by translating the Greek word *fonei* as "sound" in one instance but as "voice" in the other. The Greek words are the same across both verses: a form of *akouo* for "hear" and a form of *fonei* for "voice." Now it is true that *fonei* can also mean "sound" depending on the context, but we have already been told in verse 9:4 that it was a *voice* that Paul heard, and we are told what the very words were. Acts 26:14 tells us the voice spoke in "the

25

Hebrew language." So it cannot have been simply an inarticulate "sound" that's being referred to in Acts 9:7. Thus there is no contextual support for the NIV view that "sound" is the correct translation here.

As for "hear" versus "understand" in Acts 22:9, Christian apologists have long insisted on this distinction in order to "refute" the contradiction. The name often associated with this claim is W.F. Arndt, who was once a co-author of a widely-used Greek lexicon of the New Testament. Here is his argument:

> "The construction of the verb 'to hear' *(akouo)* is not the same in both accounts. In Acts 9:7 it is used with the genitive, in Acts 22:9 with the accusative. The construction with the genitive simply expresses that something is being heard or that certain sounds reach the ear; nothing is indicated as to whether a person understands what he hears or not. The construction with the accusative, however, describes a hearing which includes mental apprehension of the message spoken. From this it becomes evident that the two passages are not contradictory."[9]

Notice that this quotation does not come from any lexicon or grammar that Arndt has written, but from his apologetic work *Does the Bible Contradict Itself?* The apologists would have us stop there and accept Arndt's conclusion. Unfortunately for them, his explanation is not consistent with how these grammatical forms are used elsewhere in the New Testament. In fact, *akouo* can take its direct object in either the accusative or the genitive case

---

[9] W.F. Arndt, *Does the Bible Contradict Itself?* (Concordia Publishing House, 1976), pp.13-14.

with no difference in meaning. A concise rebuttal of Arndt's attempted refutation is given by Daniel B. Wallace.[10] Wallace gives several examples from the New Testament where *akouo* + genitive appears and the hearer obviously understands the meaning, as well as examples of *akouo* + accusative where little or no comprehension takes place. This usage is exactly the opposite of what Arndt would have us expect, and so the pattern on which his argument rests is found to be illusory and contrary to the textual evidence. Notice that this is not simply a difference of opinion between two experts. The case can be decided by looking into actual uses of *akouo* in the New Testament to see if the pattern claimed by Arndt holds up. It does not, and the alleged refutation fails. Wallace concludes, "Regardless of how one works through the accounts of Paul's conversion, an appeal to different cases probably ought *not* form any part of the solution."[11]

When the dust settles, the discrepancy between Acts 9:7 and Acts 22:9, between the men hearing the voice and not hearing the voice, remains as a classic case of the Bible contradicting itself, although you might not know it depending on which translation you're reading.

These examples illustrate how important it is to rely only on the most literal translations of the Bible when searching for contradictions and inconsistencies. My preference for personal use is the Revised Standard Version, and the

---

[10] Daniel B. Wallace, *Greek Grammar Beyond the Basics: An Exegetical Syntax of the New Testament* (Zondervan, 1996), p.133.
[11] If an author wanted to draw a contrast between hearing and understanding, the verb *sunieimi* was available, meaning "to understand or comprehend." It is so used in Mark 4:12: "That they might hear (*akouo*), but not understand (*sunieimi*)." Also in Luke 8:10.

particular edition I like to use is *The New Oxford Annotated Bible* published in 1973 by Oxford University Press. In this edition, you get the advantage of one of the more accurate English translations, plus the added benefits of numerous footnotes and cross-references, and a large amount of background material that helps to provide some context for the Bible passages themselves.

In the chapters that follow, unless otherwise indicated, the quoted passages from the Bible are from the KJV. This choice is driven primarily by copyright concerns. Most of the modern Bible translations are copyrighted, and quoting extensively from them could trigger concerns about exceeding the fair use limits under copyright law, not to mention payments of large sums of money to the copyright holders. The KJV, being in the public domain, is under no such limitation. As one of the more literal translations, it will serve our purposes well. But for ease of understanding, when quoting biblical passages I have replaced some of the archaic forms of the KJV to be less jarring to modern ears. For example, "whosoever believeth" will be quoted as "whoever believes;" "thou shalt" is changed to "you will," etc. None of this will change the meaning, but will only modernize the vocabulary. Occasionally, when the KJV rendering is so archaic in terms of both syntax and vocabulary as to make it misleading or incomprehensible to modern readers without major rewording, brief passages will be cited from the modern translations, such as the RSV, NASB, or NIV, and those will be noted as they occur.

Chapter 3: Rebutting the Rebuttals

I once heard a skeptic bemoan the fact that he had presented a Christian with a list of contradictions from the Bible, but the Christian had managed to refute them all. It's possible that the list he provided did not contain the strongest examples, because there are a lot of so-called contradiction lists floating around on the internet that have not had the weaker examples weeded out. But it's also possible that the contradictions were valid and the skeptic was just not sure how to rebut the alleged refutations. So before getting into the contradictions themselves, let's try to anticipate what some of the objections may be from the theologians and other guardians of religious orthodoxy. Knowing how your Christian opponents are likely to respond will help you stand your ground as you deliver your return volley.

Of course the Bible has been around for a long time, and obviously the contradictions it contains have been around for just as long. Even in the early days of the Church, many of the New Testament's difficulties were recognized, and responses were attempted. For example, the conflicting genealogies of Jesus given in the gospels of Matthew and Luke drew the attention of Augustine and other Christian apologists at least as early as the 4th century AD, and efforts were made to reconcile their inconsistencies. However, it is not always necessary to anticipate the specific Christian response to each and every contradiction in order to refute their rebuttals, because their defensive tactics fall into patterns that are easy to recognize and which can often be answered with a fairly standard set of responses. Of course, a knowledge of the specific historical, cultural, and linguistic evidence behind a particular contradiction will always make you a more formidable debater, but there are so many inconsistent passages in the Bible that no one can reasonably expect to be an expert on all of them. Even in the literature of biblical errancy, you will find contradictionists who specialize in one or two contradiction issues. For example, one contradictionist may be an expert on the discrepancies in the Jesus birth narratives, while another may focus on the misuse of Old Testament passages that allegedly foretell the coming of Jesus. But even without such specialized knowledge you can still debate with confidence, provided that you understand the weaknesses underlying the typical responses you are likely to get from the Christians.

Here then are some of the typical attempts at refutation used by Christian apologists when confronted with evidence of a biblical contradiction, and suggestions for meeting them:

The Irrelevance Defense: "The contradictions don't matter, because Christians don't base their belief on logical proof, but on faith."

This defense itself is irrelevant, because we are not usually debating how Christians came to believe the way they do. The issue is whether Christian teachings are true or not, and no doctrine can be true if it conflicts with itself. So the contradictions do matter.

Although the majority of Christians may not adopt their beliefs based on logic and evidence, most do assume that there is an underlying consistency in the Christian message, and that the message *could* be proven if necessary, even if they themselves have not looked into the matter in any detail. They may originally arrive at their belief because of non-logical motivations such as emotional needs or local and family influences, but logical consistency is important even to ordinary Christians in maintaining their belief when doubt arises, as it eventually does for many believers. In my experience, being confronted with the many contradictions in the Christian scriptures comes as a great shock to the average Christian, who had no idea that the Bible contained such difficulties, and in many cases their faith is badly shaken by this realization. Also, if the Bible, because of its contradictions, can no longer serve as the foundation of Christian belief, Christians will have to find some other authority to base their faith on. Whether that turns out to be their local preacher, a TV evangelist, popular Christian authors, or parents and friends, none of these will carry the weight that the Bible did when it was thought to be the unerring word of God. The defense of their religion will have moved to less powerful authorities – mere humans – who will be even easier for freethinkers to challenge. So yes, the contradictions do matter, even to Christians.

The Triviality Defense: "The contradictions you cite are just trivial details. The basic biblical message of salvation through Jesus Christ is consistent."

As we move through this book, we shall see by means of many examples, that the contradictions in the New Testament undermine the most fundamental Christian doctrines such as salvation and the forgiveness of sins, the divinity of Jesus, the resurrection, and the second coming of Jesus. Each of these doctrines is covered in the succeeding chapters, and numerous conflicting verses show that there is *no* consistent message of Christian salvation given in the New Testament. So the contradictions are not limited to mere details. They strike at the very heart of the Christian message of salvation, which is the foundation of Christianity itself.

The Interpretive Defense: The Bible doesn't really mean what it says.

It is very common for the apologists to try to wiggle out of a contradiction by redefining or reinterpreting the words in a biblical passage. Often, the reinterpretation does not conform to the normal usage of the actual words and in some cases is pure invention. A general rebuttal that works in many of these cases is to invoke what I call the *2nd Peter principle*. In 2 Peter 1:20 we read that "no prophecy of the scripture is of any private interpretation." Thus, the Bible itself warns against putting one's own individual (i.e., "private") interpretation on biblical passages. You either have to accept the literal meaning of the words (with the contradictions) or you have to violate the command given in 2 Peter 1:20 - or give up the idea of biblical infallibility.

This means, for example, that those Christians who find Matthew 24:34 awkward, because it predicts the second coming within the lifetime of the "generation" listening to Jesus, cannot justifiably decide, as some do, that "generation" means something different here from its usual meaning, because that would be putting one's own interpretation on a biblical prophecy, which is forbidden by 2 Peter 1:20. If you happen to know Greek well enough to debate a specific verse on the linguistic merits, all the better. But if you don't have that level of linguistic knowledge, you don't have to give up the debate, because the burden is on the Christians to justify why their own interpretation should be taken over the literal meaning, especially when the Bible itself warns against using personal interpretation to understand its message.

A second general response to interpretive defenses by the Christians is to ask whether we skeptics are also allowed to put our own interpretation on passages from the Bible, or is interpretation only something the Christians are allowed to do, and then only for the difficult passages? If the difficult verses can be interpreted symbolically or metaphorically to get out of the difficulty, then can't we also interpret any Bible verse at all symbolically to mean something different from what it seems to say? Once you open the door to personal interpretation, then there's no stopping us from interpreting the whole theological structure – from the virgin birth to the resurrection to heaven and hell – as being purely a symbolic or metaphorical representation of theological ideas, and not literal truth.

The False Facts Defense: Unsupported historical, cultural, or linguistic assertions to explain away the contradictions.

It is quite common for Christian apologists to try to refute a contradiction by supplementing the biblical text with historical or linguistic "facts" which are not facts at all, but are merely assertions based on no independent evidence. This is another case where shifting the burden of proof back to the Christians will be fruitful. Do not ever accept this type of defense without asking for the supporting evidence to back it up.

A good example of this type of invalid defense occurs with respect to the contradictions in the timing of Jesus's crucifixion. The gospel of John disagrees with the other three gospels on what time of day Jesus was hung on the cross. A well-known defense of the Christians is to assert that John's gospel uses "Roman time," while the other gospel authors are using the customary Jewish timekeeping standard. This defense is so widely accepted that it even makes it into some Bible editions as a footnote. But if you bring up this contradiction and are told by your opponent that "John's using Roman time, duh!" don't just say "Oh, OK" and give up. Instead ask, "How do you know John is using Roman time? Does it say that in the Bible?" (Of course it doesn't.) "And even if he were, how do you know Roman time was measured any differently from the way the Jews measured time?" (It wasn't.) The burden of proof is now on the Christian, who of course has no evidence at all to back up his assertion. Note that merely citing another Christian apologist who makes the same assertion is not evidence. Evidence in this case would be, for example, quotations from Roman authors who measure time in the way claimed by the apologists, plus some internal evidence in John's gospel that would support the notion that all the time references are based on the Roman system of measuring the hours of the day. As we shall see later, in chapter 5, the evidence actually shows that "Roman time" is no different from Jewish time, and the gospel of John really does contradict the other gospels on this point.

The linguistic version of this tactic is often used by Christians who have a smattering of Greek, but are nowhere close to being authorities on the language. However, this does not stop them from declaring authoritatively that "when *fonei* is used with the genitive case it means 'sound' but with the accusative case it means 'voice'" in order to escape the contradiction we looked at earlier between Acts 9:7 and 22:9. Again, the key to maintaining control of the debate is to keep the burden of proof on your opponent and require that they justify their assertion. How do they know that the Greek case endings are used in this way? Can they produce a Greek grammar that backs them up? Probably not. As always, simply producing another Christian who agrees with them is not corroborating testimony. We are not counting votes, but weighing evidence. In order to rebut this type of attempted refutation you don't have to know Greek yourself, you just have to insist that your Christian opponent produce some independent evidence that their claims about language usage are true.

The Harmonizing Defense: Claiming that apparently conflicting verses do not really conflict, because they both could have occurred.

The form of the argument is this: "If one verse says A happened and another verse says B happened, then there is no contradiction, because both A *and* B could logically have occurred." Sometimes this requires the invention of additional details C, D, and E in order to create a context in which both A and B could simultaneously be true. Often we are told that these additional details "might" have happened, even though the Bible does not mention them. In this case the additional details serve to subsume the conflicting verses into a single context that harmonizes them and thus eliminates the contradiction. The apologists claim that the apparently conflicting verses are actually describing different aspects of the same event, and therefore do not contradict each other.

This defense differs from the false facts defense in that the additional details which are invented are specific to the event being considered, and do not relate to general historical or linguistic knowledge. This is a particularly frustrating tactic for contradictionists to rebut. The Christian seems to escape from the trap and there often appears to be no way of getting him back in. There are good responses to this defense, but the exact rebuttal may vary depending on the specific situation. We can distinguish three subtypes of this category:

Harmonizing Defense – Case 1: The Christians are right.

Yes, sometimes they are, and in these cases both verses could be true without contradicting each other. This is because the context which the apologist invents is plausible, even if unstated, based on other information or knowledge that we might have. For example, in Luke 23:25, Barabbas, the man whom Pilate released, is identified as guilty of "insurrection and murder." In John 18:40, however, he is described as a "robber." Christians respond that there is no contradiction here, because Barabbas "might have been" a robber as well as an insurrectionist and murderer. In this case, they are correct. Not only is it possible for the same person to be both a murderer and a robber, we know from experience that a person who commits one criminal act is likely to have committed others. The verses can therefore be harmonized if we make this very reasonable assumption. It is both *possible* and *plausible* to think that Barabbas the robber might also have been Barabbas the murderer. So we should not insist on this pair of verses as a real contradiction. However, if we had been told that Barabbas was both a murderer and a saint, we would justifiably insist on this as a contradiction, because it is very *implausible* that the same person would be both, even though it is *possible* to conceive of a murderer becoming a saint, or vice versa. We would therefore insist that the author provide some additional detail to show us how the same person could be both. In those circumstances the situation becomes more like case 3, described below.

However, even as it stands, there is certainly a difference, if not a contradiction, between the description of Barabbas in the two verses, and we may legitimately ask why the two gospel authors chose to describe Barabbas in such different words. The more differences there are in two versions of a story, the more justified we are in concluding that the authors are not really telling the same story, and that there is a conflict in the overall meaning conveyed to the reader. There is no sharp line to tell us when the differences between two stories become so great that we cannot believe both are true. It is a matter of degree.

Harmonizing Defense – Case 2: Even with the expanded context, the verses are found to be contradictory when viewed in the light of other Bible passages.

At first glance, these types of verses appear to fall into the subtype identified in Case 1, i.e., they appear to be compatible with each other, if certain reasonable assumptions are made. But on searching further in the Bible, we find additional details which make it impossible for both to be true. These cases represent a true contradiction, and not a mere difference in description. Thus, the harmonizing defense fails in these situations, but they do require some additional research in order to uncover the related details from elsewhere in the Bible to prove the incompatibility.

An example of this type occurs in the descriptions of the first meeting of Jesus with his disciples after his resurrection. The question is: "How many of his disciples were present at that first post-resurrection meeting?" Luke 24:33 says there were eleven, but John 20:24 tells us that Thomas was absent, so there must have been only ten disciples present, contradicting Luke. (Judas Iscariot, the betrayer, was no longer with the group, so the total number of disciples remaining was eleven.) The standard apologetic response would be to say that there is no contradiction, because Luke and John are describing two different meetings. This would seem to be a reasonable assumption at first glance, but is it consistent with the rest of the internal evidence?

It is not, and we can show that this is indeed a *bona fide* contradiction. We know this because John goes on to describe two additional meetings between the risen Jesus and his disciples, one eight days later (John 20:26) and one subsequent to that at the Sea of Tiberias (John 21:1). John then tells us that the appearance at the Sea of Tiberias was "the *third* time that Jesus showed himself to his disciples, after that he was risen from the dead." (John 21:14). This rules out the possibility that Luke is describing a fourth meeting. And we know that Luke 24:33 cannot be describing a meeting that occurred *after* the one at the Sea of Tiberias, because the timeline in Luke's description shows that his meeting must have occurred in the night, or wee hours of the next morning, following the discovery of the empty tomb on the first Sunday after the crucifixion. Phrases such as "that same day" (Luke 24:13), "the same hour" (24:33), and "as they thus spoke" (24:36) confirm this timeline, as well as 24:21 where we learn "today is the third day since these things were done." Thus, Luke 24:33 and John 20:24 must be describing the same meeting between Jesus and his disciples, i.e., the first post-resurrection meeting that Jesus had with the disciples. And they contradict each other as to how many disciples were present at this meeting. If they were describing different meetings, then the Sea of Tiberias meeting would have been the fourth, and not the third, so would thus contradict John

21:14. So there is a contradiction either way. Thus, what appeared at first glance to be possibly a mere difference in the descriptions of two separate meetings, is now confirmed as two conflicting accounts of how many disciples were present at one meeting.

Harmonizing Defense –Case 3: Statements which require the reader to make extreme and implausible assumptions about the context of the action, in order to avoid a direct contradiction.

Again, the apologists attempt to treat these contradictory pairs of verses as mere differences like we saw in case 1. The distinction, however, is that in order to do so, they have to invent highly unlikely events that are found nowhere in the Bible, to create a context that will barely accommodate both verses. Because these additional contextual details are so implausible, they are not credible enough to overcome the ordinary context implied by the actual passages. This type of defense is very challenging and frustrating to rebut. The apologists believe they have refuted the contradiction. The contradictionist disagrees, but often has trouble finding the flaw in the argument.

Before looking at an example, let us clarify the logic involved here. The are two different ways that a pair of passages may contradict each other: 1) the *concrete meanings* of the words themselves may conflict, or 2) the meanings and images *conveyed to the reader* may be contradictory, even when the words themselves are only "differences." Christian apologists typically will not recognize the second type as contradictions, and and we may not be able to persuade them otherwise. But the real test of a contradiction in a literary work is how it is understood by the reader. If a reasonable reader, making

39

normal contextual assumptions, would understand the passages as contradictory, then a contradiction exists. If the Bible were a mathematical treatise we would apply a different standard, but it is not.

An example will help to make this clear. Mark 15:21, as well as Matthew 27:32 and Luke 23:26, all say that a passerby named Simon of Cyrene was pressed into service to carry Jesus's cross to the place of crucifixion. But John 19:17 says that Jesus went out "bearing his cross"[12] to the place where he was crucified. So who carried the cross? Simon or Jesus? There would appear to be a contradiction in these two versions of the story.

However, I've heard an apologist claim that there is no contradiction here. His argument was that Jesus started out carrying his own cross, but grew tired, at which point Simon of Cyrene was compelled to carry it the rest of the way. So both versions are true and the contradiction disappears.[13]

Of course, there is nothing in the text itself to suggest that any such handoff happened. The apologist just made up these extra details in order to harmonize the conflicting stories. But what image would normally be conveyed to the reader by these different versions? On reading the accounts

---

[12] NASB and RSV have "bearing his *own* cross," and NIV has "carrying his *own* cross," capturing a nuance missing from the KJV.

[13] This same apologist argued that no contradiction could be counted unless the language of each conflicting version expressly excluded the other. As for example, "Jesus went out bearing his own cross from start to finish, and no one else carried it for him, not even part of the way." Such language is legalistic, not literary, and it is not at all reasonable to expect that any actual writer would express himself in such a manner. By this standard, no writer would ever contradict another.

in Mark, Matthew and Luke, would a reader naturally understand that Simon picked up the cross from an exhausted Jesus, even though nothing of the sort is stated or implied in the passage? Would that same reader, based on John 19:17, naturally understand that Jesus grew tired and needed help from a bystander, even though there is no hint in the text that any such thing occurred? The answer of course is no. The images conveyed to the mind of a normal reader contain nothing of this handoff of the cross in mid-journey. The reader would naturally understand the version of Mark/Matthew/Luke to mean that Simon carried the cross the entire way – and if anything different was meant, it was the responsibility of the author to add whatever details were necessary to convey the accurate image. Similarly, a reader would naturally understand "bearing his own cross" to mean that Jesus carried his cross the entire way to the place of the crucifixion. (There are additional grammatical reasons for believing this as well, but that is a different type of argument which does not relate to the issue under discussion.)

The point is this: If the wording is such that the natural understanding of the reader would result in contradictory images being presented to his or her mind, then the passages are *contradictory in effect*. And if additional details or context are required in order to resolve those contradictions, it is the *responsibility of the author* to provide such details and context in order to avoid being charged with a contradiction. The burden is on the author to write clearly and completely enough to prevent any such misunderstanding, if that indeed is what is occurring. If the author does not add such details or context, we as readers can legitimately assume that the meaning we have understood is the one that the author actually intended to convey, and if that leads to contradictory messages, then we can reasonably charge the author with a contradiction.

The most absurd example I have seen of this particular tactic was on a Christian website where the apologist tried to reconcile the inconsistent accounts of Judas's death. In Matthew 27:3-5 we are told that Judas hanged himself, but in Acts 1:18 we find that after falling in his field he burst open in the middle and all his bowels gushed out. The apologist argued that there is no conflict at all between these two versions. Obviously (to him), Judas hanged himself, but was cut down (by some unidentified person) before he died. He then lived long enough to later die from falling in the field. Here, the act of cutting Judas down before he died from the hanging was pure invention on the Christian's part. There's no basis for it whatsoever in the biblical texts, or in any other sources. Certainly if such an extraordinary set of circumstances had actually happened, we would reasonably expect the author to mention it. The fact that he did not, justifies our conclusion that the authors did not have any such details in mind, and that the conflicting versions do in fact contradict each other, given the normal assumptions about meaning and context that any reasonable reader would make.[14] The more unlikely or implausible the additional details are, the less credibility we give them, and the more the burden is on the author to include them in his narrative.

---

[14] Another version, subject to the same objections, says that Judas hanged himself on a tree that overlooked a cliff, but the branch broke while he was still alive, whereupon he fell down the cliff, into his field, where he burst open and his bowels gushed out. Again, these details are pure invention on the part of the apologist.

The Absence of Evidence defense

"Absence of evidence is not evidence of absence." This is a classic Christian defense that says just because you don't see it mentioned in the biblical text doesn't mean it didn't happen. Actually, this one can sometimes be a valid defense. It still doesn't mean that you can make up imaginary events to get out of a contradiction. But it does mean that if one Bible author describes an event, while another makes no mention of it, we can't consider that to be a *bona fide* contradiction. The fact that it is absent from an author's narrative is not evidence that it did not happen.

Take for example the fact that the virgin birth is not mentioned anywhere in the gospels of Mark and John, nor in the letters of Paul. Does this conflict with Matthew and Luke who describe in detail Mary's conception without the benefit of human assistance? No, it doesn't. There's nothing in Mark and John to contradict those particular stories in Matthew and Luke. It's just that Mark and John don't deal with that period of Jesus's life. As between Matthew and Luke, however, there are *bona fide* contradictions, because they both tell of Jesus's birth and early childhood, but present details that are mutually incompatible.

While not contradictory, such omissions can still present a problem for Christian apologists. Although there is not a *logical* contradiction between Matthew/Luke on the one hand, and Mark/John on the other, we certainly are justified in asking why, if Jesus was born of a virgin, Mark and John chose to remain silent on the matter, and why there is no mention of such an idea in the letters of Paul. It certainly seems very puzzling that they would ignore such an extraordinary event which would undoubtedly add to the persuasiveness of their message, if indeed they were aware of it at all. The argument then becomes one based on plausibility and likelihood, rather than on strict logical consistency. Is it plausible that Mark and John would have left out the claim that Jesus was born of a virgin, with the Holy Spirit as his father, if indeed they were aware of and believed in such a claim?

The Bottom Line

Most Christian "refutations" of biblical contradictions will fall under one of the categories described above. By using the suggested counter-arguments, you can usually rebut these defenses rather easily. The categories in this chapter suggest general approaches, and can be used to rebut Christian refutations for a wide variety of contradictory passages. In the chapters which follow, we'll provide additional extended discussion on some of the more well-known contradictions that have received attention from the apologists, and we'll provide some more detailed points that you can use when arguing these specific cases.

Chapter 4: Contradictions in the Stories of Jesus's Birth

When was Jesus Born? Contradictions between Matthew and Luke

While the gospels of Mark and John mention nothing about Jesus's birth, both Matthew and Luke describe his birth and early childhood. Historical events cited in Matthew place Jesus's birth in 4 BC or earlier. But different historical events cited in Luke place the birth in 6 AD. Obviously, both cannot be correct.

You can usually tell how damaging a Biblical contradiction is to the Christian position by how numerous and extreme are their attempts to refute it. By that measure, the two contradictory accounts of when Jesus was born must represent a direct hit on the fortress of Biblical infallibility, for this contradiction has given rise to numerous attempted refutations from the Christian camp. Many amateur historians and linguists have desperately attempted to find, create, or reinterpret historical evidence to bring these conflicting accounts into harmony and preserve the supposed infallibility of the Bible. To delve into the full range of historical and linguistic evidence would take us far beyond the scope of this book, but the outlines of the argument can be concisely summarized. For a more detailed treatment, I highly recommend the excellent article by Richard Carrier,[1] "The Date of the Nativity in

---

[1] The 5th edition (2006) of this article is available online at *www.infidels.org/library/modern/richard_carrier/quirinius.html*.

Luke." See also L. Michael White, *From Jesus to Christianity*, pp.32-34. After all the evidence is considered, the contradiction remains. But the Christians are right to be worried, because if we can't trust the Biblical accounts of the beginning of Jesus's life, how can we ever believe the even more fantastic accounts of its end?

What the Gospel Authors Tell Us

Both Matthew and Luke tie the birth of Jesus to historical events that can be independently verified and dated. According to Matthew's version, the birth of Jesus occurred during the reign of Herod the Great, king of Judea. (Matthew 2:1) Herod had three sons who were also called Herod (Herod Archelaus, Herod Antipas, and Herod Philip), but we know that Matthew was referring to Herod the Great because he states specifically that after Herod's death, during Jesus's childhood, he was succeeded by his son Archelaus. (Matthew 2:22) So there is no doubt that Matthew is telling us Jesus was born during the reign of Herod the Great, shortly before Herod's death. Herod the Great is known to have died in 5 or 4 BC, so in Matthew's version, Jesus must have been born in 4 BC or at most a year or two before, but certainly not later.

Luke gives us an entirely different date, which has to be at least ten years later. Luke places Jesus's birth during the time of a Roman census that was conducted when Judea passed from being a client state under the empire to direct Roman rule. As Luke tells us, this census was taken when the Roman official Quirinius was governor of Syria. (Luke 2:1-2) Quirinius became governor of Syria in 6 AD after Archelaus was deposed by the Romans. So the interval between Matthew's date of 4 BC and Luke's date of 6 AD gives us a discrepancy of at least 10 years between the two gospel versions of Jesus's birth. There is no way to reconcile this contradiction.

The Historical Evidence

The dates of Herod's death and Quirinius's governorship are not seriously questioned by reputable scholars. Herod's death in 4 BC is supported by the Jewish historian Josephus, who places the death during the time when Quintilius Varus ruled Syria.[2] From Roman records we know that Varus was governor of Syria between 6 and 3 BC.[3] Josephus also reports that Herod died shortly after a lunar eclipse,[4] and the astronomical data point to such an eclipse in the region during the year 5 BC.[5] So Herod's death is established as either 5 or 4 BC. If, as Matthew tells us, Jesus was born during Herod's reign, that pins down Jesus's birth to 4 BC or earlier, but not too much earlier, because Herod's massacre of the babies was limited to those who were two years old and under (Matthew 2:16), so a date between 6 BC and 4 BC for Jesus's birth is established as a consequence of Matthew's narrative.

Turning now to the historical data relating to Luke's version, Quirinius's rule over Judea began in 6 AD following the exile of Herod's son Archelaus. This marks the beginning of direct Roman rule over Judea, which includes the cities of Jerusalem and Bethlehem, but not Nazareth, which lies to the north in Galilee. Josephus tells us that Archelaus was banished in the tenth year of his

---

[2] Josephus, *Antiquities of the Jews.* Book XVII, chapters 5-8.
[3] See Carrier's article for citations of ancient sources regarding the dates of Roman governors.
[4] Josephus, *Antiquities,* Book XVII, 6.4-8.1.
[5] Eclipse data available from NASA at
http://sunearth.gsfc.nasa.gov/eclipse/LEhistory/LEhistory.html#3

reign, which had begun after Herod's death in 4-5 BC. After the banishment of Archelaus, Quirinius "came himself into Judea, which was now added to the province of Syria, to take an account of their substance, and to dispose of Archelaus's money; but the Jews, although at the beginning they took the report of a taxation heinously, yet did they leave off any further opposition to it, by the persuasion of Joazar, who was the son of Beethus, and high priest; so they, being over-persuaded by Joazar's words, gave an account of their estates, without any dispute about it."[6]

This "taking account of their substance" can only be the same Roman census that Luke identifies as the reason for Joseph and Mary traveling to Bethlehem: "Now in those days a decree went out from Caesar Augustus, that a census be taken of all the inhabited earth. This was the first census taken while Quirinius was governor of Syria." (Luke 2:1-2) (NASB) The census would have been required because the province would now be under direct Roman administration, and it was important for the empire to have an idea of what resources were available for imperial revenue. During the reign of Herod, and of Archelaus as well, there would have been no need for a Roman census, since it was the king's responsibility to figure out how to extract the required revenue from his subjects. According to Luke, Jesus was born while Joseph and Mary were in Bethlehem for this census. Thus, a birth year of 6 AD follows from Luke's gospel – in other words, ten years later than the year that Matthew arrives at.

---

[6] Josephus, *Antiquities,* Book XVIII, 1.1.

Christian Attempts to Resolve the Contradiction

Obviously at least one of the gospel accounts is wrong. But believers in the infallibility of the Bible do not give up that easily. There have been many attempts to explain away the discrepancy, but none of the explanations is consistent with what is known about Roman history and custom during that time period.

It has been claimed by some Christian apologists that Quirinius may have been governor of Syria during an earlier period that is not described in the historical records. Might there have been a different census conducted by the Romans during the time of Herod the Great that Luke was referring to? If so, this would put Luke's census during the reign of Herod, and line up with the dates from Matthew. But the answer is "No." This proposed scenario is implausible on several grounds[7]:

1) There is no evidence that Quirinius ever served as governor of Syria before the time reported by Josephus. Indeed, no Roman governor ever governed the same province twice, and it is undisputed that Quirinius was in fact governor of Syria in 6 AD.

2) There is no evidence of any other Roman census being conducted in Judea before the one of Quirinius. Luke is clear and explicit about it being a Roman census, so no other type of census would resolve the contradiction. Before the exile of Archelaus, Judea was a tributary kingdom, and as we have seen, the Romans did not take the trouble to conduct a census in kingdoms which they did not directly administer. Instead, the client king was responsible for collecting whatever taxes and tribute were due.

---

[7] See Carrier's article for detailed sources.

3) The previous Roman governors of Syria back to 12 BC are known through Roman sources: Marcus Titius (12-9 BC), Sentius Saturninus (9-6 BC), Quintilius Varus (6-3 BC). This gets us up to the point where Herod the Great is already dead, and outside the time specified by Matthew. Quirinius did not achieve consular rank until 12 BC and thus would not have qualified for the position any earlier than that year according to Roman law and custom.

Thus, the idea that there was a previously unknown and unrecorded census during a previously unknown and unrecorded governorship of Quirinius before the death of Herod the Great is pure speculation and unsupported by any facts.

So the contradiction remains. Matthew puts the birth of Jesus during or before 4 BC, while Luke puts it in 6 AD. At least one of these accounts has to be wrong. And it's entirely possible that both are wrong. Either way, the inescapable conclusion is that the Bible is in error as regards the birth year of Jesus.

A Postscript

Commentators often cite Luke 1:5 as corroboration that Jesus was born during the reign of Herod the Great, consistent with Matthew. Luke 1:5 begins, "There was, in the days of Herod, the king of Judaea . . ." and goes on to tell the story of Zacharias and Elizabeth, parents of John the Baptist, after which we have the angel Gabriel's visit to Mary. But it's not absolutely certain that Luke is saying that John and Jesus were born at nearly the same time. In fact, Luke's description leaves open the possibility that there were some years between the birth of John and the birth of Jesus, because Luke never tells us exactly when Mary became pregnant with Jesus. However, for our purposes it doesn't matter anyway, because if Luke means Herod the Great in 1:5, and if he intends us to understand that Jesus's birth followed shortly thereafter, then Luke contradicts himself, for as we have seen, the census of Quirinius is still placed in 6 AD. So there would then be a ten-year discrepancy within Luke's gospel itself. In verse 1:5 Luke probably means Archelaus, not Herod the Great. As Carrier points out,[8] Archelaus also called himself Herod, and his coinage identified him only by the name of Herod. So if Luke meant Archelaus in 1:5, then Luke is internally consistent with regard to his timeline for Jesus's birth, although he remains in conflict with Matthew.

The Genealogy of Jesus: Conflicting Accounts from Matthew and Luke

In order for Jesus of Nazareth to be taken seriously as the Jewish Messiah, he had to be, or at least claim to be, a direct descendant of king David. Accordingly, Matthew and Luke both trace the ancestry of Jesus back to David and beyond. Matthew takes the genealogy as far as Abraham, while Luke goes all the way back to Adam. While sharing some common elements, the two versions of the genealogy differ considerably. From Abraham down to David they are largely consistent, with only a couple of discrepancies. But from David down to Jesus's father Joseph, the two lists have almost nothing in common, and do not even agree from which of David's sons Joseph is descended. Matthew traces the line from David's son Solomon through 27 generations to Joseph. (Matthew 1:6-16) Luke, on the other

---

[8] Carrier, "The Date of the Nativity in Luke," website cited above in note 1.

hand, has Joseph descending from David's other son Nathan, through 42 generations. (Luke 3:23-31) Almost none of the names are the same between the two lists; it is only the father/son combination of Shealtiel and Zerubbabel that appears on both of them.

The Hebrew genealogies in the Old Testament book of Chronicles provide a third source for comparison. 1 Chronicles 3:10-19 takes the Solomon line of David's descendants down through Shealtiel in 19 generations, with a list that shares several names with Matthew's, although Matthew gets from Solomon to Shealtiel in only 15 generations. After Shealtiel, the Chronicles list becomes more difficult to follow and appears to lose any remaining correspondence with Matthew's list. Chronicles does not list the descendants from David's son Nathan, whose name appears only in passing. (This Nathan is not to be confused with Nathan the prophet, who plays a prominent role during the reigns of David and Solomon.). Thus, there is no Chronicles list to compare with Luke's version of the genealogy. Of course, the author of Chronicles makes no attempt to tie any of these names to Jesus, who was born centuries after that list was compiled.

It is obvious that these versions of Jesus's ancestry cannot all be right. Once again, as we saw in the case of Jesus's birth year, either Matthew or Luke must be wrong. Quite likely they are both wrong, given that Chronicles has yet a third version of the line from David through Shealtiel.

It can be quite confusing to try to sort all this out just from the biblical text, so here is a chart for easy comparison. You can see that in many respects the three sources do not agree with each other. This list uses the Revised Standard Version translation of the names:

ABRAHAM TO DAVID

Matthew	Luke	Chronicles
Abraham Isaac Jacob Judah Perez Hezron Ram Amminadab Nahshon Salmon Boaz Obed Jesse David *(14 generations)*	Abraham Isaac Jacob Judah Perez Hezron Arni Admin Amminadab Nahshon Sala Boaz Obed Jesse David *(15 generations)* (The various Greek manuscripts vary widely for Luke 3:33 in listing the names between Hezron and Nahshon. Also, the KJV has Aram in place of Arni and Admin.)	Abraham Isaac Israel (=Jacob) Judah Perez Hezron Ram Amminadab Nahshon Salma Boaz Obed Jesse David *(14 generations)* *from 1 Chronicles 1:28-2:15*

The Atheist's Introduction to the New Testament

DAVID TO JOSEPH (husband of Mary, and Jesus's earthly father):

Matthew	Luke	Chronicles
David	David	David
Solomon	Nathan	Solomon
Rehoboam	Matatha	Rehoboam
Abijah	Menna	Abijah
Asa	Melea	Asa
Jehosaphat	Eliakim	Jehoshaphat
Joram	Jonam	Joram
Uzziah	Joseph	Ahaziah
Jotham	Judah	Joash
Ahaz	Simeon	Amaziah
Hezekiah	Levi	Azariah
Manasseh	Matthat	Jotham
Amos	Jorim	Ahaz
Josiah	Eliezer	Hezekiah
Jechoniah	Joshua	Manasseh
Shealtiel	Er	Amon
Zerubbabel	Elmadam	Josiah
Abiud	Cosam	Jehoiakim
Eliakim	Addi	Jeconiah
Azor	Melchi	Shealtiel
Zadok	Neri	
Achim	Shealtiel	*(From 1 Chronicles 3:10-19.)*
Eliud	Zerubbabel	
Eleazar	Rhesa	
Matthan	Joanan	
Jacob	Joda	
Joseph	Josech	
(27 generations)	Semein	
	Mattathias	
	Maath	
	Naggai	

Contradictions in the Stories of Jesus's Birth

Matthew	Luke	Chronicles
	Esli Nahum Amos Mattathias Joseph Jannai Melchi Levi Matthat Heli Joseph (42 generations)	

As you can see, Matthew and Luke do not agree on the number of generations from David to Joseph. They do not agree on any of the names except Shealtiel and Zerubbabel. They do not even agree on the name of Joseph's father or grandfather. Given these discrepancies, we can give Matthew and Luke no credence at all regarding Jesus's ancestry or his supposed relation to the house of David. The lists give every appearance of having been compiled by human writers, with partial and imperfect knowledge, using whatever sources they had available, of varying reliability and completeness, combining varying degrees of fact and legend, and no little imagination. What they do *not* look like is the literal and complete word of a perfectly omniscient supernatural god, or the words of writers who had access to direct communications from such a god. The obvious explanation is that both Matthew and Luke, working independently and without any knowledge of the other's efforts, both tried to substantiate Jesus's claim to be the messiah by showing his ancestry from the royal house of

55

David. To accomplish this, they made up ancestors where no such relationship existed. Unfortunately for their credibility, each came up with a result that contradicts the other, and together they once again shatter the notion of biblical infallibility.

Possibly Luke chose to begin this part of Jesus's genealogy with David's son Nathan rather than starting with Solomon, because Solomon's line includes the accursed Jehoiakim, whose offspring were barred by God from ever "sitting upon the throne of David, and ruling any more in Judah." (Jeremiah 22:30) A messiah who claims to be the heir to the throne of David obviously could not claim descent from Jehoiakim. Matthew deals with this by simply omitting Jehoiakim from his ancestral list, while Luke switches to an entirely different branch of David's family tree. Observe that the author of 1 Chronicles 3:15, having no foreknowledge of Jesus or his claims to be the messiah, includes Jehoiakim in his proper sequence.

Notice also that Matthew's arithmetic is wrong. He tells us that "all the generations from Abraham to David are fourteen generations; and from David until the carrying away into Babylon [Jechoniah] are fourteen generations; and from the carrying away into Babylon unto Christ are fourteen generations." (Matthew 1:17) Abraham to David is indeed fourteen generations, and Solomon to Jechoniah is also fourteen, but Matthew can only get fourteen for the final period by counting Jechoniah twice, because from Shealtiel to Jesus is only thirteen generations.

We might wonder what is the point of giving us the genealogy of Jesus when Jesus is supposed to have been born of a virgin, so that Joseph would not be his "real" father anyway. This is very awkward to explain if one accepts both the virgin birth doctrine and Jesus as the messiah, for the messiah is supposed to come from the house of David: "Behold, the days come, saith the LORD, that I will raise unto David a righteous Branch, and a king shall reign and prosper, and shall execute judgment and justice in the earth. In his days Judah shall be saved, and Israel shall dwell safely." (Jeremiah 23:5-6)

The genealogical accounts in both Matthew and Luke accommodate the virgin birth by adding disclaimers. Luke speaks of Jesus as "being *as was supposed* the son of Joseph, who was the son of Heli." (Luke 3:23) Matthew has Jacob as the father of "Joseph *the husband of Mary*, of whom was born Jesus, who is called Christ." (Matthew 1:16) So neither Matthew nor Luke states directly that Joseph is Jesus's actual father, but if he is not, then Jesus is not descended from the house of David, and the whole point of the elaborate genealogy is lost – in which case the genealogies are not only contradictory, but irrelevant as well.

By contrast, Paul, who seems unfamiliar with the virgin birth legend, writes that Jesus was descended from David *"according to the flesh."* (Romans 1:3) Paul's position causes some additional awkwardness for those who hold to the virgin birth doctrine. The Greek phrase in the quotation from Paul is *kata sarka*, which is literally "according to the flesh." But some translators try to salvage the virgin birth by fudging the translation of Romans 1:3. For example, the NIV translation of the same verse refers to Jesus "who *as to his human nature* was a descendant of David" thus downplaying the fleshly inheritance.

Christian Rebuttal

One common answer given by the Christians to these two different versions of Jesus's ancestry is to claim that

Matthew lists the ancestors of Joseph, while Luke traces the ancestry of Mary. Typically, this argument is simply asserted without any supporting evidence. The apologists argue that Luke's genealogy *must* be that of Mary, because otherwise there would be a contradiction. Well, yes, there would be, and in fact there is.

The simplest way to refute the "genealogy of Mary" defense is simply to ask: "Does it say that in the Bible?" No, it doesn't. Both of the genealogies end with Joseph. Neither claims to be the genealogy of Mary. And both versions specifically mention Joseph as the endpoint of their lists. Identifying Luke's version as the genealogy of Mary was actually a rather late invention (15th century) so if we really are supposed to see Mary's ancestry in Luke's list, it seems that it wouldn't have taken over a thousand years for them to come up with this explanation. Even the Catholic church rejects this line of argument: "It may be safely said that patristic tradition does not regard St. Luke's list as representing the genealogy of the Blessed Virgin."[9]

But we don't have to rely on the Catholic fathers for a refutation of the claim that Luke gives us Mary's genealogy. Luke 1:36 describes Elizabeth as a relative (*sungenis*) of Mary. Elizabeth was descended from Aaron (Luke 1:5) which means she is a member of the priestly tribe of Levi, as is corroborated by the fact that she is married to Zacharias, a Hebrew priest. Given her relation to Elizabeth, and the tribe of Levi, it is implausible that Mary, the mother of Jesus, would trace her ancestry back through David, who was of the tribe of Judah. So the idea that Luke is giving us Mary's ancestry is undermined by the additional

---

[9] "Genealogy of Christ," in *The Catholic Encyclopedia,* online at *http://www.newadvent.org/cathen/06410a.htm*

information he gives us about Mary's relation to Elizabeth. Remember that Luke himself makes no claim to be presenting Mary's genealogy, but Joseph's. Tracing Joseph's lineage back to king David at least serves the purpose of supporting Jesus's claim to be the messiah, but there would be no purpose served by giving us Mary's family tree.

Finally, there have been some efforts to reconcile the two lists by claiming that Matthew has intentionally left out some names and is speaking figuratively, so that for example, a phrase such as "Jeconiah was the father of Shealtiel," would mean that Jeconiah was an ancestor of Shealtiel, but not necessarily his immediate father. Matthew supposedly did this in order to conform to some numerological requirement to fit the genealogy into multiples of seven. As we have seen, he didn't even achieve this goal, because the last group of names only comes to thirteen. Also, even granting him the leeway to collapse the list in this way, he still has different names than Luke, so this argument gets the Christians nowhere. And are we to believe that Matthew was so afflicted with obsessive compulsive disorder that he would tamper with God's unerring truth just to satisfy his urge to come up with a neatly symmetrical numerical pattern?

The Bottom Line

Matthew and Luke present starkly conflicting lists of Jesus's and Joseph's ancestors. The genealogies contradict each other in many respects, and are inconsistent with the listing in Chronicles. There is no evidence that Luke's genealogy is that of Mary, and there is convincing internal evidence that it is not that of Mary. Because of these conflicts, the listings cannot all three be correct, and therefore at least two of the lists, more likely all three, must be incorrect, demonstrating again that the Bible is in error.

No room in the inn? More contradictions in the Jesus birth stories

The conflicting birth years and the conflicting genealogies are not the only problems with the New Testament accounts of Jesus's early years. The stories of Matthew and Luke contradict each other in other respects as well. Remember the famous Christmas story of the shepherds coming to Jerusalem and visiting the baby Jesus in the manger because there was no room for them in the inn? This version of the story is from Luke. "And she brought forth her firstborn son, and wrapped him in swaddling clothes, and laid him in a manger; because there was no room for them in the inn." (Luke 2:7) And the shepherds, who were informed of the event by an angel, "came with haste, and found Mary, and Joseph, and the babe lying in a manger." (Luke 2:16)

Matthew has no such story about a manger. Instead, he has the three magi (not shepherds) visit the baby Jesus in a house: "When they saw the star, they rejoiced with exceeding great joy. And when they had come into the house, they saw the young child with Mary his mother, and fell down, and worshipped him." (Matthew 2:10-11) A house is not a manger, in Greek or any other language. Merriam-Webster defines a manger as "a trough or open box in a stable designed to hold feed or fodder for livestock."

Luke's version is suspect in any case, because it seems very odd that a resident of Nazareth, which is in Galilee, would be required to register for a census in Judea, where

Contradictions in the Stories of Jesus's Birth

Bethlehem was located. The purpose of the Roman census in Judea was to take stock of the region's wealth for purposes of taxation. Recall that Galilee was at this point still ruled semi-autonomously by Herod's other son Antipas, and so was not part of the census. Unless Joseph owned property in Bethlehem, there would be no reason for him to take part, and certainly no reason for Mary to accompany him on the journey. "It is improbable that any Roman census would have required a man to report to the home of his ancestors. Such a procedure would have been almost as impracticable in Roman times as it would be in our own, and the Roman state was interested in a man's property, not in his pedigree."[10] However, if Joseph did own property in Bethlehem (an assumption not warranted by Luke's story), it is very difficult to explain why he and Mary stayed in a stable, instead of at his own property.

But speaking of Nazareth, was it really the home of Joseph and Mary? Luke says that Joseph came from Nazareth to Bethlehem for the census (Luke 2:4) and that Nazareth was "their own city" (Luke 2:39), and indeed Nazareth is where Luke says the angel Gabriel appeared to Mary and advised her that she would conceive a child by the holy spirit. (Luke 1:26) But Matthew says that after returning from Egypt, "when he heard that Archelaus did reign in Judaea in place of his father Herod, he was afraid to go there; notwithstanding, being warned of God in a dream, he turned aside into the parts of Galilee. And he came and dwelt in a city called Nazareth: that it might be fulfilled which was spoken by the prophets - He shall be called a Nazarene." (Matthew 2:22-23)

---

[10] *The Interpreter's Bible* (Abingdon Press, 1952), vol.8, p.50.

This is the first mention of Nazareth in Matthew's gospel, and it gives the distinct impression that Joseph had no previous connection with the town of Nazareth, but was only going there to fulfill a prophecy, not because that was his home. (Never mind that there is no such prophecy in the Old Testament, as we shall see later.) Indeed, it is implied from Matthew's account that Joseph would have returned to Judea except for the fact that Archelaus was ruling there. Matthew gives no hint that there was any previous connection between Joseph and Nazareth, and gives no explanation for how Joseph and Mary came to be in Bethlehem when Jesus was born. Thus, Matthew's account strongly implies that Joseph and his family were not from Nazareth, conflicting with Luke's direct statements that they were.

Even now we have not yet exhausted all the contradictions between the two birth stories of Jesus, for Matthew's story of the escape to Egypt is directly contradicted by Luke's gospel. Matthew tells a very dramatic tale of Joseph fleeing with his family to Egypt after Jesus is born, in order to escape the murderous plans of King Herod. The king planned to massacre all the infants in Bethlehem to make sure of destroying the baby Jesus. (Matthew 2:13) As we have seen, even after Herod's death, Matthew tells us that Joseph was afraid to go back to Jerusalem or anywhere else in Judea, because Herod's son Archelaus was still ruling.

But Luke's sequence of events never mentions Egypt, and instead has the family proceeding from Bethlehem directly to Jerusalem. So Luke says the family went to Jerusalem, and Matthew says they avoided it out of fear. And the omission of the Egyptian journey from Luke's version cannot be explained by claiming that Luke simply left it out, because his timeline leaves no room for any such trip. Here's the sequence of events, which clearly shows the incompatibility of the two stories:

Matthew:

- Jesus is born in Bethlehem. (Matthew 2:1)
- From Bethlehem, Joseph and family flee to Egypt to escape massacre by Herod. (Matthew 2:14)
- While in Egypt, and after Herod's death, Joseph is told in a dream to return to the land of Israel, "for they are dead which sought the young child's life." But on the way, he has another dream, giving opposite advice, and warning him against going to Judea, and so he is afraid to go there, because Herod's son is still ruling. (Matthew 2:20-22)
- The family goes instead to Nazareth, and not to Jerusalem. (Matthew 2:23)

Luke:

- Joseph and Mary travel from Nazareth to Bethlehem for Jesus's birth. (Luke 2:4)
- After 8 days Jesus is circumcised. (Luke 2:21)
- After the days of purification pass (33 days according to Leviticus 12:2-4) Jesus's parents bring him from Bethlehem to Jerusalem "to present him to the Lord" (Luke 2:22)
- Finally, they return to Nazareth, but continue to go to Jerusalem every year while Jesus is growing up, even though by Matthew's chronology Archelaus continued to rule Judea until Jesus was about 10 years old. (Luke 2:39-41)

Thus, there is nowhere in Luke's timeline where a journey to Egypt will fit. By Luke's account, Jesus was taken to Jerusalem when he was only 41 days old. So any trip to Egypt would have had to occur during those 41 days, because after that time, Jesus and his family regularly went to Jerusalem, at a time when Matthew tells us they were avoiding the city for the ten years of Archelaus's reign. Matthew 2:14-15 also says Jesus was in Egypt "until the death of Herod." So not only does the trip not fit into Luke's 41 day time window, it suffers from the same discrepancy we saw with regard to the birth year. Matthew places it ten years before Jesus was born according to Luke's version. So the flight to Egypt is not merely omitted by Luke; it is positively precluded by his sequence of events. Therefore, if Matthew's chronology is correct, Luke's must be wrong, and vice versa.

Mary, the Unclean Virgin

Luke's reference to "their days of purification" (2:22) seems very odd, because the requirement as given in Leviticus 12:2-4 refers to the days during which a woman is unclean after giving birth. "The LORD said to Moses, 'Say to the people of Israel, if a woman conceives, and bears a male child, then she shall be unclean seven days; as at the time of her menstruation, she shall be unclean. And on the eighth day the flesh of his foreskin shall be circumcised. Then she shall continue for thirty-three days in the blood of her purifying; she shall not touch any hallowed thing, nor come into the sanctuary, until the days of her purifying are completed.'" (Leviticus 12:1-4) (RSV)

Luke's implication is that Mary, after giving birth to Jesus, was considered subject to the same purification law as other Jewish mothers, and thus was unclean during the time specified in Leviticus. "Hallowed" means "holy," and if anything is holy in Christian doctrine it would be Jesus himself. Are we to imagine that Mary did not touch her baby during these 41 days because she was prohibited from touching anything holy? Yet this is the requirement that Luke's story implies. In fact, we are told directly that Mary "wrapped him in swaddling cloths and laid him in a manger" (Luke 2:7), so there is no doubt that she did touch him, in violation of the law stated in Leviticus. There are many Church writings that proclaim the absolute purity of the Virgin Mary, [11] so Luke's off-handed comment about the days of purification, implying that Mary was unclean after giving birth to Jesus, is at odds with a central teaching of the Catholic Church, and with the belief of many non-Catholics as well.

Notice that Luke also mistakenly refers to "their purification" rather than "her purification." The purification law as stated in Leviticus is only for the mother, not the whole family. The commandment from Leviticus refers to "*her* purifying," so to speak of "*their* purifying" indicates that the author was either careless with his pronouns, or was not entirely familiar with Jewish rituals. The KJV translation of this verse corrects Luke's mistake and replaces "their" with "her," but the Greek text has "their," and it is so translated by most of the modern versions.

The Bottom Line

We have seen that Matthew and Luke give two widely divergent accounts of the birth of Jesus. The birth dates are

---

[11] For a list of writings proclaiming the "absolute purity" of Mary, see the article "Immaculate Conception," in *The Catholic Encyclopedia,* online at
http://www.newadvent.org/cathen/07674d.htm

in conflict. The genealogies contradict each other. The circumstances of the family's lodging in Bethlehem (house versus manger) conflict. Matthew and Luke conflict on whether Nazareth is actually the home town of Joseph. And there are inconsistent versions of where the family traveled after Jesus's birth.

These contradictions are clear and unambiguous and cannot be reconciled with each other. At least one, and probably both of these accounts, are fictional stories made up to justify the later claims by Jesus's followers that he was the long-awaited Jewish messiah. Whatever the motivation, we are forced into the inescapable conclusion that the Bible is in error in its portrayal of the early years of Jesus's life.

Chapter 5: Contradictions in the Crucifixion and Resurrection Stories

Without the crucifixion and resurrection of Jesus, there would be no Christian religion. Contradictions concerning Jesus's birth certainly undermine any claims that the Bible is infallible, but the foundations of Christianity do not hang on the question of whether Jesus was born in 4 BC or 6 AD. By contrast, the resurrection is absolutely essential to the theological edifice that was founded in Jesus's name. The Nicene Creed which was adopted by the Council of Constantinople in 381 AD, and has represented the core of Christian belief ever since, proclaims that Jesus "was crucified also for us under Pontius Pilate, suffered and was buried, and the third day rose again according to the Scriptures." Paul was well aware of the importance of the resurrection for the new faith: "If Christ be not risen, then is our preaching vain, and your faith is also vain." (1 Corinthians 15:14)

To be sure, there are individuals who consider themselves Christians who do not believe in the literal truth of the resurrection. These individuals may admire the sayings of Jesus and revere him as a great moral teacher, and may even call themselves "Christians," but without the belief in the resurrection, this type of admiration is no different from that bestowed upon the likes of Socrates and Marcus Aurelius, who have similar admirers. I only mention this to make clear what we mean when we say that the crucifixion and resurrection are the key elements of the Christian religion. For our purposes, Christians are those who believe in the doctrine. (This may be one of the few statements in this book that most Christians would agree with.)

The story of Jesus's entry into Jerusalem, his betrayal by Judas Iscariot, his trial before Pontius Pilate, his death on the cross, and his resurrection on the third day, is told by all four of the gospel writers. Given that these events occurred over the space of only a few days, in a small, well-defined location, and that two of the gospels (Matthew and John), if we believe the early church tradition, were written by Jesus's own disciples who would have been present and eyewitnesses as the events unfolded, you would expect these four accounts to agree not only in the basic gist of the story, but also in the details. However, if you expected that, you would be disappointed, for the four gospel narratives contradict each other in many essential facts, to the point of undermining the credibility of the whole story.

Imagine a courtroom proceeding where there are four witnesses. All four give testimony relating to the same event. But one says the event took place at night and another says it was during the day. One says it was at nine o'clock and another puts it at twelve o'clock. One says that two men were present, another says only one man was present. One says Smith drove the getaway car, another testifies that Jones drove it. And all of it is hearsay, because none of the witnesses were actually at the scene. How would a competent court deal with these witnesses? How would they stand up under cross-examination, if indeed they were even allowed to testify? Most importantly, how much credibility would an impartial jury give to such witnesses? Now suppose that these witnesses are all trying to establish that a dead man came to life again. Most likely they would all be charged with perjury, and any lawyer who relied on such witnesses to prove the case would no doubt receive a

Contradictions in the Crucifixion and Resurrection Stories

stern rebuke from the court. Yet this is the type of testimony the gospels offer to persuade us that Jesus of Nazareth was crucified and rose from the dead.

Suppose then, upon cross examination, these witnesses tried to reconcile their testimony by the same devices that apologists use when trying to reconcile the conflicting stories in the Bible. One witness might say, "It's true that I said we left at nine o'clock and my buddy said we left at noon, but I was using Pacific time while he was using Eastern standard time." Or, "Sure I said Smith drove the getaway car, and my co-defendant said Jones drove it. But what I meant was that Smith started out driving it, then stopped, switched places with Jones, and then Jones drove the rest of the way." Would such defenses convince anyone? Of course not. We would ask, "Why didn't you mention that the first time around when you testified?" You'll recall that this is case 3 of the harmonizing defense that we discussed in chapter 3. The addition of fantastic and implausible details to harmonize conflicting stories does not work, because any reasonable writer would have included these details in the original story if the true picture depended so heavily on them.

The sheer number of inconsistencies contained in the resurrection stories prevents us from including an extended discussion for each one. But the words of the gospels speak for themselves. The contradictions are so direct and straightforward, that little additional commentary is necessary to show that if any of the witnesses is telling the truth, the others must be mistaken.

Crucifixion Contradictions:

How long would Jesus be in the tomb before rising again?

- "Three days and three nights in the heart of the earth" (Matthew 12:40)
- But all the gospels have Jesus in the tomb for only *two nights* (Friday & Saturday) and *one full day* (Saturday), having been crucified on Friday and rising before sunrise on Sunday morning. The gospel narratives contradict Jesus's own prediction. Mark, for example, tells us that Jesus was crucified on the day of "preparation, that is, the day before the Sabbath" [i.e., Friday]. (Mark 15:42), and that he was gone when the women came to his tomb "very early in the morning the first day of the week" [i.e., Sunday] (Mark 16:2) In other words, he was already gone when the sun came up on Sunday, so Sunday shouldn't count even for a partial day.

How many times would the cock crow before Peter denied Jesus three times?:

- Twice (Mark 14:30,72)
- Once (Matt 26:34,74; Luke 22:34, 60; John 13:38; 18:27)

This may seem easy to refute as a contradiction, because it could simply be argued that the rooster did crow twice, but Mark was the only one to mention the second crowing. However, when all the details are put together, it becomes clear that the rooster cannot have crowed twice in Mark without contradicting Luke, as well as Matthew and John. If you'll recall the examples from chapter 3 on rebutting the refutations, this one falls under Case 2 of the harmonizing defense, where the Christians deny that a contradiction exists, but additional circumstances within the biblical text show that the two verses are in fact incompatible.

Immediately[1] after Peter's third denial in Mark 14:72, the rooster crows for the second time, meaning that it must have crowed for the first time before the third denial. However, in Luke 22:34, Jesus says that "the cock *shall not crow this day*" before Peter denies three times that he knows Jesus. Jesus's words in Luke mean that the rooster cannot crow at all before the third denial. John 13:38 has similar wording: "The cock shall not crow, till thou hast denied me thrice." But Mark's version requires that it crow once *before* the third denial in order for the second crowing to follow "immediately" after the third denial is spoken. So crowing once versus crowing twice is a real contradiction, and cannot be refuted by claiming that Luke, Matthew, and John simply omitted one of the instances of the rooster crowing.

Did Jesus want his disciples to fight back when the Romans came to arrest him?:

- Yes: "He that has no sword, let him sell his garment, and buy one." (Luke 22:36) "And they said, Lord, behold, here are two swords. And he said to them, 'It is enough.'" (Luke 22:38)
- No: "Lord, shall we strike with the sword? And one of them struck the slave of the high priest and cut off his right ear. But Jesus said, 'No more of this!'" (Luke 22:49-51) (RSV) "Put up again your sword into its place: for all that take the sword shall perish with the sword." (Matthew 26:52)

---

[1] The KJV omits "immediately," which appears in the Greek as *euthus*. The modern translations (NASB, RSV, NIV, etc.) include it.

Who carried the cross to the place of crucifixion?

- Simon of Cyrene carried the cross for Jesus. (Mark 15:21; Matthew 27:32; Luke 23:26)
- Jesus carried his own cross. (John 19:17)

Refer back to the discussion on this one in chapter 3, starting on page 40.

What time of day was Jesus crucified?

- At the third hour. (Mark 15:25)
- More than three hours later, for at the sixth hour John has Jesus still with Pilate before the Jewish crowd. (John 19:14)

Jewish time of day began counting at dawn, i.e., around 6 a.m. So, the third hour of Mark is "about 9 a.m." And the sixth hour of John is "about noon."[2] The apologists like to claim that John was using a different standard of time, namely "Roman time," which in their view explains the discrepancy. The NASB translation even has a footnote to John's "sixth hour," saying it is "perhaps 6 a.m. Roman time." If true, this would help to bring John's account into synch with Mark's, as it would then still be possible for Jesus to be crucified at the third hour in Jewish time, as Mark says.

BUT: The "Roman time" argument is totally implausible and unsupported by the text or by what we know about the Roman system of reckoning time. There is nothing in John's text to indicate that he had "Roman time" in mind. John's gospel was not written in Rome nor for a Roman audience. The best scholarly opinion places its composition

---

[2] *The New Oxford Annotated Bible.* pp. 1237 and 1314.

in Ephesus (in present-day Turkey) or somewhere in Syria.[3] If anyone was going to use "Roman time" it would have been Mark, because there is good reason to believe that Mark's gospel may have actually been written in Rome.[4] But what really puts this argument to rest is the fact that the Romans, too, reckoned time from sunrise, and not from midnight.

The Romans had one set of hours for the daylight period beginning at sunrise, and another set for the night hours, beginning at sunset. They did not start counting time at all from midnight. So the sixth hour in Roman time would still be around noon, and not 6 a.m. "The Romans had a twenty-four-hour day and night, just as we do but, in a manner different from ours, daylight was divided into twelve hours and darkness into another twelve. . . . In writing of the Roman day it is convenient to treat the first hour of day as lasting from six to seven o'clock in the morning and the twelfth as lasting from five to six in the evening. In fact, however, a daylight hour at the winter solstice in Rome was about forty-five minutes long, at the summer solstice about an hour and a quarter."[5] Thus, there is no support for the idea that the Romans started counting the hours of the day at midnight, which would be required if the "Roman time" argument had any chance of reconciling John's crucifixion account with the other gospels.

For more evidence against the "Roman time" argument, see also "Reckoning Time in Ancient Rome,"[6] by Joseph

---

[3] White, *From Jesus to Christianity,* p.310.
[4] Ibid., p.233.
[5] J.P.V.D. Balsdon, *Life and Leisure in Ancient Rome* (McGraw-Hill, 1969), pp. 1-2.
[6] Joseph Francis Alward, "Reckoning Time in Ancient Rome." Online at *http://sol.sci.uop.edu/~jfalward/Ancient_Rome.htm.*

Francis Alward. Alward's essay includes a number of quotations from ancient Roman authors, confirming that they counted the time of day starting with sunrise. Furthermore, elsewhere in John's gospel whenever he mentions the time of day, normal Jewish time seems to be a better fit for the events he's describing. (e.g., John 1:39; 4:6; 4:52-53) In none of these other passages is there any hint that the author of John is using anything other than standard Jewish time, which as we've seen, is no different from Roman time. The idea that he meant anything else, is not based on any evidence, either from internal Biblical sources, or from external Roman sources. Therefore, the discrepancy between Mark and John on the time of Jesus's crucifixion is a real contradiction.

What words were inscribed and hung over Jesus on the cross?

- "The king of the Jews." (Mark 15:26)
- "This is Jesus, the king of the Jews." (Matthew 27:37)
- "This is the king of the Jews." (Luke 23:38)
- "Jesus of Nazareth, the king of the Jews." (John 19:19)

The gist of these is substantially the same, and apologists would suggest that the reported differences involve only minor details. But it would seem that divinely inspired eyewitnesses would have all agreed on the exact wording that appeared on the sign. Given how short the inscription is, it is amazing that the gospel witnesses cannot even agree on what it said. John's gospel adds that the charge was posted in three languages: Hebrew, Latin, and Greek. (John 19:20) Some of the Greek manuscripts for Luke 23:38 also mention the three languages.

Contradictions in the Crucifixion and Resurrection Stories

How many robbers reviled Jesus as he hung on the cross?
- Both of the robbers reviled Jesus. (Matthew 27:44; Mark 15:32)
- Only one of the robbers reviled him. (Luke 23:39-42)

One apologist has claimed that these can be reconciled by assuming that both robbers at first reviled Jesus, but one then changed his mind and asked to be remembered in his kingdom. This attempt at a refutation is in the same class with trying to claim that Simon of Cyrene picked up the cross after Jesus grew tired of carrying it. In order for both to work, new assumptions have to be made which are highly implausible, and not supported in the biblical text. Furthermore, it is not reasonable to believe that any writer would leave out such an amazing conversion on the cross, especially when he knew, as Luke surely did, that leaving these details out would result in a contradiction with Mark's gospel, which Luke used as a source. See the general discussion of this type of attempted refutation in chapter 3, under case 3.

What were Jesus's last words on the cross?
- "My God, my God, why hast thou forsaken me?" (Mark 15:34) "And Jesus cried with a loud voice, and gave up the ghost." [Literally, "expired."] (Mark 15:37)
- "My God, my God, why hast thou forsaken me?" (Matthew 27:46) "Jesus, when he had cried again with a loud voice, yielded up the ghost." (Matthew 27:50)
- "'Father, into thy hands I commend my spirit: and having said thus, he gave up the ghost." [Literally, "expired," as in Mark 15:37.] (Luke 23:46)
- "When Jesus therefore had received the vinegar, he said, 'It is finished': and he bowed his head, and gave up the ghost." (John 19:30)

Here again, apologists follow their usual tactic of claiming that no contradiction exists, but that Jesus uttered all of these words while on the cross, and each author picked only a portion of what he said to report to us. But this is clearly contrary to the plain meaning expressed by the passages, because each of the reported utterances is followed by the statement that Jesus "expired" or "yielded up his ghost," indicating that the words are meant to represent his last words on the cross. Furthermore, the quoted words are so different from each other in tone, that it is impossible to believe they could have been spoken by the same person. The despairing tone of "My God, my god, why hast thou forsaken me?" rules out any compatibility with the resigned acceptance of the words reported by Luke, nor does it fit in with the overall calm and confident demeanor of Jesus as he appears in Luke's gospel.

Who were the first to come to Jesus's tomb on Sunday?

- Mary Magdalene, Mary mother of James, and Salome (Mark 16:1)
- Mary Magdalene and "the other Mary" (Matthew 28:1)
- Mary Magdalene, Mary mother of James, Joanna and "the other women" (Luke 24:10)
- Mary Magdalene only (John 20:1)

When did they come?

- "When the sun had risen." (Mark 16:2) (RSV)
- "When it was yet dark." (John 20:1)

When the women got there, where was the stone that had covered the entrance to the tomb?

- They saw an angel descend and roll away the stone. (Matthew 28:2)

Contradictions in the Crucifixion and Resurrection Stories

- The stone had already been rolled away when they arrived. (Mark 16:4; Luke 24:2; John 20:1)

Who did the women see at the tomb?

- One young man sitting on the right, inside the tomb. (Mark 16:5)
- The angel who rolled away the stone, sitting outside the tomb. (Matthew 28:2)
- *Two* men appeared in dazzling apparel inside the tomb. (Luke 24:4)
- Peter and the other disciple see only the linen wrappings and the face-cloth. But after they leave, Mary Magdalene, standing outside the tomb, looks in, and sees *two* angels in white, one at the head and one at the foot of where the body had been lying. Then she turns around and sees Jesus, but does not recognize him at first. (John 20:11-18)

Surely no one who reads these conflicting testimonies with an open mind can come away with the feeling that these four writers deserve any credibility at all for their stories. An impartial jury would put no faith in any of them, nor in the events they purport to relate. Given the contradictions, the accounts cannot possibly all be true. If John is right about Jesus carrying his own cross, then Matthew, Mark, and Luke are wrong. If Matthew and Mark are right about both robbers reviling Jesus on the cross, then Luke is wrong. If Luke is right about the last words of Jesus on the cross, then Mark, Matthew, and John are wrong. Obviously, someone is wrong, and on multiple counts, because these conflicting stories undercut each other. And yet Jesus's death and resurrection are the cornerstone of the entire Christian religion. And speaking of the resurrection, what do our four witnesses have to say about that? Is their

77

testimony of that event any more reliable than that of the crucifixion?

The Post-Resurrection Appearances Of Jesus

Surprisingly, the raising of Jesus from the dead is not described anywhere in the gospels or indeed in the entire New Testament. There is not a single word from any eyewitness, or even any hearsay testimony, relating how the dead Jesus rose up and walked out of his tomb. What we have instead are stories about an empty tomb, and then appearances by Jesus at various places afterwards. But these stories are fraught with inconsistency and contradiction just as much as the crucifixion story. Here's a summary of what each of our witnesses has to say about the alleged post-resurrection appearances of Jesus:

MARK:

In the version of Mark's gospel represented by the oldest manuscripts (ending with 16:8), Mark does not tell us of any appearances by Jesus after the crucifixion. The verses from 16:9 to 16:20 only appear in later Greek manuscripts, and are generally believed by Bible scholars to have been added by a later editor. However, in this addendum, we are told that Jesus did appear several times after his crucifixion, although the times and locations of the appearances are not given. According to these verses, Jesus first appears to Mary Magdalene (16:9) who goes to tell the disciples what she saw, but the disciples don't believe her. Then Jesus appears "in another form" (we are not told what that means) to two unnamed disciples as they are walking out into the country (16:12). These two report it to the other disciples,

Contradictions in the Crucifixion and Resurrection Stories

but again the others don't believe. Then Jesus appears directly to the eleven disciples as they are eating (16:14).[7] And after speaking to them he is received up into heaven and sits down at the right hand of God (16:19).

MATTHEW:

In Matthew's version of Jesus's post-resurrection appearances, he meets Mary Magdalene and the other Mary as they are leaving the tomb to go tell the disciples what they had found. (28:9) He instructs them to tell the disciples they should leave for Galilee and meet him there (28:10). We know it was only the women who met him in verse 9, and not any of the male disciples, because the Greek pronouns are feminine gender. The eleven disciples proceed to a mountain in Galilee where they see Jesus, but even then some are doubtful. (28:16-17)

LUKE:

Luke tells us that on the same day that the women (Mary Magdalene, Joanna, Mary mother of James, and the "other" women) found the empty tomb, Jesus approaches two of his followers as they walk on the road to Emmaus, but they don't recognize him (24:16), even though he walks with them for the rest of their journey. When they finally recognize him that night at supper, he suddenly vanishes. (24:31) These two followers return to Jerusalem and find the eleven disciples gathered together (24:33). Before the two travelers tell their own story, they are told that "The Lord has risen indeed, and has appeared to Simon." (24:34) Suddenly, Jesus appears to them all, and the disciples are

---

[7] These appearances bear a general similarity to those described in Luke 24:13-37.

"terrified and affrighted, and supposed that they had seen a spirit." (24:36-37). Jesus tells them to remain in the city [Jerusalem] until they are "clothed with power from on high." (24:49) (RSV) The disciples then remain in Jerusalem and are "continually in the temple." (24:52-53) In Luke's version, which is continued in the book of Acts, Jesus continues to appear over a period of 40 days after his resurrection (Acts 1:3). During this time, Jesus "commanded them that they should not depart from Jerusalem, but wait for the promise of the Father." (Acts 1:4)

JOHN:

At the tomb, Jesus first appears to Mary Magdalene, but initially she doesn't recognize him. (20:14) On the evening of that same day, he appears to the disciples while they are indoors, hiding "for fear of the Jews." (20:19) But Thomas was not there, and did not believe when it was reported to him later. (20:24-25) After eight days, Jesus appears to them again, while shut up inside, and Thomas is present. (20:26) Later, after an unspecified time, Jesus appears again to the disciples at the Sea of Tiberias (Sea of Galilee) but they don't recognize him until the disciple whom Jesus loved points it out. (21:7) This is given as "the third time that Jesus showed himself to his disciples, after that he was risen from the dead." (21:14)

A comparison of the details in the four post-resurrection stories quickly reveals that they are in serious conflict with each other:

Contradictions in the Crucifixion and Resurrection Stories

Did Jesus instruct the disciples to meet him in Galilee?

- Yes: Jesus told the women on their way back from the empty tomb: "Be not afraid: go tell my brethren that they go into Galilee, and there shall they see me." (Matthew 28:10)
- No: In Luke's version, as we have noted, Jesus twice tells the disciples to remain in Jerusalem. (Luke 24:49 and Acts 1:4)

Geographical note: Jerusalem is not in Galilee. Jerusalem was in the territory of Judea, and Galilee was a region lying to the north of Judea. Jesus's hometown of Nazareth was in Galilee.

Note that the apologists cannot fall back on their usual line of saying that both are true. Because Jesus ordered the disciples to "not depart from Jerusalem" (Acts 1:4) a meeting in Galilee is thus precluded. You cannot go to Galilee from Jerusalem if you are forbidden to depart.

Where did the disciples first meet the resurrected Jesus?

- They met him in *Galilee*, per his previous instructions. (Matthew 28:16-17)
- They met him in *Jerusalem*. (Luke 24:33-36)

The disciples follow the instructions previously given to them in each version, with Luke having them remain in Jerusalem, and Matthew describing a meeting in Galilee.

How many disciples were present when Jesus first met them after the resurrection?

- On Sunday, the day of the resurrection, Jesus's first appearance to the disciples was to the full group of *eleven*. (Matthew 28:16-17; Luke 24:33 – but in different places)

- On Sunday, the day of the resurrection, Jesus's first appearance to the disciples was only to *ten* of them, Thomas being absent. (John 20:24) Jesus didn't meet Thomas until eight days later. (John 20:26)

Once again, the discrepancy cannot be resolved by claiming that two separate meetings are being described. The meeting described in Luke 24:33 must be the same as the one in John 20:24. The reasons were given earlier in chapter 3, in the illustration of case 2, on pages 37-39.

Where were the disciples when Jesus ascended to heaven?

- Jesus ascended to heaven as the disciples were seated *indoors*. (Mark 16:14-19)
- Jesus ascended to heaven when the disciples were *outdoors*, on the Mount of Olives. (Acts 1:9-12)
- Jesus ascended to heaven when the disciples were *outdoors*, at Bethany. (Luke 24:50-51)

When did Jesus ascend to heaven?

- Jesus ascended to heaven on the first night following the resurrection. (Luke 24:51)
- Jesus ascended to heaven at least 40 days after the resurrection. (Acts 1:3, 9)

There is a clear contradiction between the ascension as told in Luke's gospel versus the story told in Acts. In the gospel, the appearances following the resurrection form a continuous narrative that unfolds on the Sunday of the resurrection, extending into that night, and perhaps into the wee hours of the following morning, at which time Jesus "was parted from them, and carried up into heaven." (Luke 24:51) Some ancient manuscripts simply say that he "departed from them," and omit the part about being carried

Contradictions in the Crucifixion and Resurrection Stories

up into heaven. However, this departure is still seen as his ascension into heaven, because in Acts, the author says that in his first book (i.e., the gospel of Luke) he told us about the life and teachings of Jesus "until the day in which he was taken up." (Acts 1:1-2) So the parting at the end of Luke's gospel is indeed Jesus's ascension into heaven, occurring less than 24 hours after his resurrection.

But Acts 1:3 tells us that Jesus remained on the earth for at least forty days after his crucifixion presenting himself by "many proofs," after which he was lifted up and taken away by a cloud. (Acts 1:9) So there is a forty day discrepancy in the dates for the ascension in Luke and Acts.

Eyewitness accounts?

These conflicting details about the resurrection and ascension are even more troublesome for those fundamentalists who believe that the gospels were actually written by those men under whose names they appear, for two of them – Matthew and John – are taken to be among the twelve that Jesus chose as his closest disciples. Under this presumption then, Matthew and John would both have been among the eleven (or ten) to whom Jesus appeared, so should agree on whether Thomas was present or not at the first meeting. They should also agree on whether Jesus first met the disciples cowering inside for fear of "the Jews" (John) or on a mountain in Galilee (Matthew). Of course serious Bible scholars do not believe these gospels were actually written by the disciples Matthew and John, but many fundamentalist Christians still hold such a belief. Those who take this view of gospel authorship, are hard pressed to explain why these two men, who were both supposedly eyewitnesses to the same events, are in such disagreement with each other over what actually happened.

The Disbelieving Disciples

There is another puzzling theme that recurs throughout these stories, which is often overlooked. Repeatedly we are told that the disciples do not believe it when they hear that Jesus has risen, and even when they see Jesus after the crucifixion they do not always recognize him.

- When the women returning from the tomb told the eleven that Jesus had risen, their words "seemed to them as idle tales, and they believed them not." (Luke 24:11)
- "And when they saw him they worshiped him, but some doubted." (Matthew 28:17)
- When Thomas was told of Jesus's appearance to the other ten, he replied, "Except I shall see in his hands the print of the nails, and put my finger into the print of the nails, and thrust my hand into his side, I will not believe." (John 20:25)
- In Mark the two travelers who had seen Jesus "went back and told the rest, but they did not believe them." (Mark 16:13) (RSV)
- "For as yet they [the disciples] knew not the scripture, that he must rise again from the dead." (John 20:9) [Even though Jesus himself told them so in Mark 8:31, Matthew 16:21 and Luke 9:22.]
- At the empty tomb, Mary Magdalene "turned herself back, and saw Jesus standing, and knew not that it was Jesus . . . supposing him to be the gardener." (John 20:14-15)
- As for the two travelers in Luke, "while they were talking and discussing together, Jesus himself drew near and went with them. But their eyes were kept from recognizing him." (Luke 24:15-16) (RSV)
- At the Sea of Tiberias, "Jesus stood on the shore: but the disciples knew not that it was Jesus." (John 21:4)

Contradictions in the Crucifixion and Resurrection Stories

What are we to make of these doubtful disciples who disbelieved reports of the resurrected Jesus and who failed to recognize their teacher? Simply this: That those who walked with Jesus and followed him most closely during his ministry, had no expectation at all that Jesus must die and be raised from the dead in order to save people from their sins. Jesus's death at the hands of the Romans came as a complete shock to them. And once Jesus was dead, the disciples had no expectation that he would rise again. Otherwise they would not have reacted so skeptically to the initial reports of his resurrection. Furthermore, their failure to recognize the resurrected "Jesus" raises the suspicion that some of his supporters rounded up an imposter who resembled Jesus, to play the role of the "resurrected Jesus" and start the rumor that he had risen from the dead. How else can we explain the fact that so many of his closest followers failed to recognize their teacher in these alleged post-resurrection appearances?

If there is any objective basis to these stories at all, it suggests that Jesus did not teach the resurrection as part of his doctrine; that he was viewed by his followers merely as the Jewish messiah, who would recapture Jerusalem from the Romans, and become the earthly king of the Jews at the head of a revitalized nation of Israel. But when the Romans crucified him and put an end to Jesus and his messianic movement, his followers who survived him were faced with either disbanding the movement or finding a new rationale for continuing it. By the time the gospels were written, the doctrine of the resurrection represented the redefined purpose of the Jesus movement, and Jesus's transition from earthly Hebrew messiah to the heavenly savior of Jews and Gentiles alike. The doctrine of the resurrection was then promoted by reinterpretations of Hebrew scripture, and not by the actual teachings of Jesus that his disciples were familiar with. A full discussion in support of this view would take us far beyond the scope of the present work, but it is more plausible than the fantastic and unbelievable stories told by our four gospel witnesses.

Chapter 6: Sin, Forgiveness and Salvation

Some more liberal Christians may concede that the New Testament does indeed contain some minor factual discrepancies, but they consider these to be trivial details, and continue to insist that the basic message of salvation in the New Testament is still clear and consistent: For many Christians, that message is encapsulated in John 3:16: "For God so loved the world, that he gave his only begotten Son, that whoever believes in him should not perish, but have everlasting life." The passage continues: "For God sent not his Son into the world to condemn the world; but that the world through him might be saved. He that believes in him is not condemned. but he that believes not is condemned already, because he has not believed in the name of the only begotten Son of God." (John 3:17-18) There are few Christians who would argue with this as a summary of the basic Christian message. These Christians would say that even though the resurrection accounts may conflict in the details, they are united in proclaiming Jesus, as Christ, to have risen from the dead, as part of God's plan for the salvation of mankind. We can call this belief the orthodox doctrine. But it is not the only view of sin and salvation found in the New Testament, as we shall see. Not only the details, but the core message of salvation is contradicted again and again throughout the New Testament. To read through all 27 books from start to finish is to witness a ferocious theological debate as to who Jesus was, who is to be saved, and how salvation is to be obtained.

First, let's look at the scriptural support for the orthodox doctrine, as presented in the writings of the New Testament.

The Orthodox Doctrine of Sin and Salvation

All Have Sinned:

- "All have sinned, and come short of the glory of God." (Romans 3:23)
- "Therefore just as through one man sin came into the world, and death through sin, so also death spread to all men because they all sinned." (Romans 5:12)
- "If we say that we have no sin, we deceive ourselves, and the truth is not in us." (1 John 1:8)

Those who sin are doomed to judgment:

- "For the wages of sin is death." (Romans 6:23)
- "And when he is come, he will reprove the world of sin, and of righteousness, and of judgment." (John 16:8)
- "For we must all appear before the judgment seat of Christ; that every one may receive the things done in his body, according to what he has done, whether it be good or bad." (2 Corinthians 5:10)
- Jesus "is the one ordained by God to be judge of the living and the dead." (Acts 10:42)

Jesus died on the cross as a sacrifice for our sins:

- "Christ died for our sins according to the scriptures." (1 Corinthians 15:3)
- "For Christ also has once suffered for sins, the just for the unjust, that he might bring us to God." (1 Peter 3:18)
- "For this is my blood of the new testament, which is shed for many for the remission of sins." (Matthew 26:28)
- In Jesus "we have redemption through his blood, the forgiveness of sins, according to the riches of his grace." (Ephesians 1:7)

Sin, Forgiveness and Salvation

Salvation comes to those who believe in Jesus's death and resurrection:

- "Through his name whoever believes in him shall receive remission of sins." (Acts 10:43)
- "If you will confess with your mouth the Lord Jesus, and will believe in your heart that God has raised him from the dead, you shall be saved." (Romans 10:9)
- "For God so loved the world, that he gave his only begotten Son, that whoever believes in him should not perish, but have everlasting life." (John 3:16)
- "Believe in the Lord Jesus Christ, and you shall be saved." (Acts 16:31)
- "A man is justified by faith apart from works of the law." (Romans 3:28) (NASB)
- "I am the resurrection, and the life. He who believes in me, though he were dead, yet shall he live. And whoever lives and believes in me shall never die." (John 11:25-26)

Salvation through Jesus is for everyone – not just the Jews:

- "For there is no difference between the Jew and the Greek. For the same Lord over all is rich unto all that call upon him. For whoever shall call upon the name of the Lord shall be saved." (Romans 10:12-13)
- "There is neither Greek nor Jew, circumcision nor uncircumcision, Barbarian, Scythian, bond nor free: but Christ is all, and in all." (Colossians 3:11)
- "There is neither Jew nor Greek, there is neither bond nor free, there is neither male nor female: for you are all one in Christ Jesus." (Galatians 3:28)
- "Is he the God of the Jews only? Is he not also of the Gentiles? Yes, of the Gentiles also . . . It is one God." (Romans 3:29-30)

If the entire New Testament consisted only of these verses, the Bible would indeed present a powerful and consistent statement of the core doctrine of mainstream Christianity. You can easily imagine the above set of verses being printed on a flyer and left on your windshield or doorstep by an energetic group of young Christian activists. And many wavering individuals who have not actually read the Bible would no doubt be persuaded by such a presentation. You certainly won't find many Christians who disagree with the overall message of these passages that we've just cited.

BUT: These verses have been cherry-picked to support the orthodox doctrine. One of the stock responses from Christians when confronted with a biblical contradiction is that the passage is "taken out of context." However, it turns out that the orthodox doctrine itself *depends* on taking verses out of context. For when we consider the whole context, we see that the Bible contradicts itself again and again on the key issues of sin, forgiveness, and salvation. Looking beyond the orthodox position, here's what we find when we read a bit more broadly in the books of the New Testament:

1) God himself created sin, by establishing the Law, and without the Law, there would be no sin.
2) Salvation comes from doing good works, not just by faith in any doctrine.
3) Salvation comes from repenting of one's sins and being baptized, not just by faith or good works.
4) Some sins cannot be forgiven at all.
5) Whether to believe in Jesus is not our choice. God predetermines whether each person believes and is saved, or is condemned.

6) Jesus's message is only for the Jews, anyway, and does not apply to non-Jews.

Obviously if sin is God's doing and not our own, and if he predetermines who believes and is saved, then there is nothing we can do about our own salvation, and all the proselytizing in the world will not make a bit of difference. If you're destined to go to hell, then you're going there, no matter what you believe. In fact, you're going to be prevented from believing, because God will "harden your heart" to make sure you do not receive his message of salvation. It is a profoundly unjust arrangement, but nonetheless is supported by the Bible itself. And if the message is only for Jews anyway, then the rest of us can just go find something else to do because Jesus wasn't talking to us.

It's impossible to overestimate how profoundly damaging this is to the entire Christian religion. The orthodox view may indeed be what Christians believe, but it is impossible to support that belief by appealing to the Bible. Here are some of the New Testament passages that undermine the orthodox position, and which support an unorthodox doctrine of salvation:

An Unorthodox Doctrine Supported by the Scriptures:

1) God himself brought about sin by establishing the Law.
- "I would not have come to know sin except through the Law; for I would not have known about coveting if the Law had not said, "You shall not covet." (Romans 7:7) (NASB)

- "Through the Law comes knowledge of sin." (Romans 3:20) (RSV)
- "For until the law, sin was in the world; but sin is not imputed when there is no law." (Romans 5:13)
- "If I had not come and spoken to them, they would not have sin; but now they have no excuse for their sin." (John 15:22) (RSV) [This is Jesus speaking. And if people had no sin before he came and spoke to them, how could the purpose of his coming be to save people from their sins?]
- "The law entered, that the offence might abound. But where sin abounded, grace did much more abound." (Romans 5:20) [i.e., God established the Law in order to make man more sinful, so that God's grace and mercy for those whom he saves will be even greater.]

2) Faith is not enough. Good works are required for salvation:

- "By works a man is justified, and not by faith only." (James 2:24)
- "Faith without works is dead." (James 2:20)
- "For as the body without the spirit is dead, so faith without works is dead also." (James 2:26)
- God "will render to every man according to his deeds." (Romans 2:6) ["Deeds" here is the same Greek word translated "works" in the verses from James.]

3) Even good works and faith are not enough. Salvation comes from repenting of your sins and being baptized:

- "Unless you repent, you shall all likewise perish." (Luke 13:3) [This is Jesus speaking.]
- "And Peter said to them, 'Repent, and be baptized every one of you in the name of Jesus Christ for the remission of sins, and you shall receive the gift of the Holy Ghost.'" (Acts 2:38)

- "Repent therefore, and be converted, that your sins may be blotted out." (Acts 3:19) [Peter is the speaker.]
- "If we confess our sins, he is faithful and just to forgive us our sins, and to cleanse us from all unrighteousness." (1 John 1:9)

Jesus's parting words to the disciples say nothing about believing in his resurrection as a condition for salvation, but he does stress repentance and baptism, which was the same message preached by John the Baptist, who "prepared the way":

- "Thus it is written, and thus it behooved Christ to suffer, and to rise from the dead the third day: And that *repentance and remission of sins* should be preached in his name among all nations, beginning at Jerusalem." (Luke 24:46-47)
- "All power is given unto me in heaven and in earth. Go therefore, and teach all nations, baptizing them in the name of the Father, and of the Son, and of the Holy Ghost." (Matthew 28:18-19)

Luke 6:37 seems to have an even less strict requirement for salvation: "Judge not, and you shall not be judged. Condemn not, and you shall not be condemned. Forgive, and you shall be forgiven." By this standard, anyone who forgives others, and refrains from judging and condemning others, will escape condemnation for himself, regardless of what he believes about Jesus.

4) Some sins cannot be forgiven at all:
- "Whoever speaks against the Holy Ghost, it shall not be forgiven him, neither in this world, neither in the world to come." (Matthew 12:32) Also Mark 3:28-29.

- "Neither the immoral, nor idolaters, nor adulterers, nor sexual perverts, nor thieves, nor the greedy, nor drunkards, nor revilers, nor robbers will inherit the kingdom of God." (1 Corinthians 6:9-10) (RSV)

Refusing to forgive the sins of others is also unforgivable:

- "But if you forgive not men their trespasses, neither will your Father forgive your trespasses." (Matthew 6:15)
- "And his lord was angry, and delivered him to the tormentors, till he should pay all that was due unto him. So likewise shall my heavenly Father do also unto you, if you from your hearts forgive not every one his brother their trespasses." (Matthew 18:34-35)

5) God prevents some of us from believing in Jesus and receiving salvation.

- "No man can come to me, unless the Father which sent me draws him." (John 6:44)
- "No man can come unto me, unless it is given unto him by my Father." (John 6:65)
- "He has blinded their eyes, and hardened their heart; that they should not see with their eyes, nor understand with their heart, and be converted, and I should heal them." (John 12:40)
- "Unto you it is given to know the mysteries of the kingdom of God: but to others in parables; that seeing they might not see, and hearing they might not understand." (Luke 8:10; see also Mark 4:11-12)
- "So then he has mercy upon whomever he wills, and he hardens the heart of whomever he wills." (Romans 9:18) (RSV)
- "The god of this world has blinded the minds of them that believe not, lest the light of the glorious gospel of

Christ, who is the image of God, should shine unto them." (2 Corinthians 4:4)

In this last passage, the theologians would have us believe that the phrase "God of this world" refers to Satan. However, the Greek word used is *theos* which means "God" and is the normal word used in the New Testament to refer to God the Father. The phrase "God of this world" does not occur elsewhere in the Bible, so there is no precedent for this phrase being used to refer to Satan, or anyone other than God himself. And there is no other passage where *theos* is used to mean Satan. Satan is twice referred to as the "*ruler* of this world" in John 12:31 and 16:11, but that is hardly the same as being a god. But if Satan is the "god" of this world, then there are at least two gods, and Christianity becomes even more of a polytheistic religion than it already is. Also, blinding the minds of the unbelievers is entirely consistent with the Christian God's character, as shown by the other quotations given above.[1]

But if the "God of this world" did refer to Satan, why would God allow Satan to sabotage his whole salvation scheme by blinding the minds of unbelievers? Satan already has caused people to sin, which led to the need for salvation through Christ's crucifixion. Are we supposed to believe that God then would allow Satan to upset that plan as well, by preventing people from coming to Christ and being saved? If so, then it's a poor salvation plan and obviously a dismal failure.

---

[1] For a fuller discussion of God himself as "the god of this world," see Donald E. Hartley, "2 Corinthians 4:4: A Case for Yahweh as the God of this Age," a paper presented to the 57th annual meeting of the Evangelical Theological Society, Valley Forge PA, November 2005. Online at *http://www.rctr.org/journal/8.pdf*.

6) Jesus's message is only for the Jews of Israel:
- "I was sent only to the lost sheep of the house of Israel." (Matthew 15:24) (RSV)
- Jesus to the disciples: "Go not into the way of the Gentiles, and into any city of the Samaritans enter ye not. But go rather to the lost sheep of the house of Israel." (Matthew 10:5-6)
- The greatest commandment is addressed only to Israel: When Jesus is asked which is the greatest commandment, he answers, "The first of all the commandments is, Hear, O Israel; The Lord our God is one Lord. And you shall love the Lord your God with all your heart, and with all your soul, and with all your mind, and with all your strength: this is the first commandment." (Mark 12:28-30)
- When a Greek woman begged Jesus to expel the demons from her daughter, Jesus replied: "Let the children first be filled [i.e., the children of Israel] for it is not meet to take the children's bread, and to cast it unto the dogs." (Mark 7:27)
- Jesus says that in disputes among believers, if an offender "refuses to listen even to the church, let him be to you as a Gentile and a tax collector." (Matthew 18:17) (RSV) In other words, Gentiles (non-Jews) are considered as outside the church, which Jesus implies is a Jewish assembly.

And Christians often overlook the fact that they only get one chance for salvation. If you sin again after being saved, you're doomed:
- "If after they have escaped the pollutions of the world through the knowledge of the Lord and Saviour Jesus Christ, they are again entangled therein, and overcome, the latter end is worse with them than the beginning.

For it had been better for them not to have known the way of righteousness, than, after they have known it, to turn from the holy commandment delivered unto them." (2 Peter 2:20-21)
- "For if we sin willfully after that we have received the knowledge of the truth, there remains no more sacrifice for sins, but a certain fearful looking for of judgment and fiery indignation." (Hebrews 10:26-27)
- "For it is impossible for those who were once enlightened, and have tasted of the heavenly gift, and were made partakers of the Holy Ghost, and have tasted the good word of God, and the powers of the world to come, if they shall fall away, to renew them again unto repentance; seeing they crucify to themselves the Son of God afresh, and put him to an open shame." (Hebrews 6:4-6)

Salvation through faith or works?

The issue of salvation through faith or works is a long-standing controversy which deserves an additional comment. The apologists claim that there is no contradiction between James and Paul on whether we are saved by works or faith. Usually they achieve this by asserting that God expects both, and that a person who has true faith will also be motivated to do good works. So, according to this argument, you would never find a person who had true faith but failed to also do good works. But the real question is whether faith *alone* is enough to achieve salvation, or are good works (i.e., obedience to the law) *required* in addition to faith in Jesus's resurrection?

The passages cited above (page 89) under the heading of the orthodox doctrine are unequivocal in stating that whoever believes in Jesus *will be saved*. There are no limitations or additional requirements given. James, by contrast, explicitly says that faith alone is *not* sufficient. "By works a man is justified, and not by faith only." (James 2:24) It cannot be convincingly argued that James takes the position that *true* faith will always, as a matter of course, be accompanied by good works. If this were the case, there would be no need for him to make his argument. To say that "faith by itself, if it has no works, is dead," implies that it is possible to have faith without works. Not just that someone may *claim* to have faith without doing good works, but actually have it. That James is not talking about mere lip service to faith is shown by verse 2:19b: "Even the demons believe - and shudder." He is talking about true belief in the true God, of the kind that even the demons have because they know God's power. And yet, James says even this belief is not enough – in contrast with Acts 10:43, Romans 10:9, John 3:16, Acts 16:31, and John 11:25-26, all of which say that belief in Jesus is sufficient for salvation. And in Romans 3:28 Paul explicitly allows that faith *can* exist without being accompanied by works of the law, and that this faith alone is enough to justify a person in the sight of God: "A man is justified by faith apart from works of the Law." (NASB) Thus, the apologetic argument that good works will automatically follow true faith, finds no support from the two antagonists in the debate, James and Paul. Their positions do indeed contradict each other, as the plain reading of their words would suggest.

Many years after Paul and James wrote, Martin Luther came down strongly on the side of faith alone as the only path to salvation. His argument, in brief, is that salvation pertains to a person's soul, which is of a spiritual nature. But works of the law are, by definition, carried out in the material world, which is inferior to the spiritual nature of man, and will eventually pass away. Therefore, works performed in the material world can have no possible effect on the higher spiritual condition of a person's soul. All good works can be performed by hypocrites as well as by God's elect, so these acts cannot possibly be a deciding factor in who will be saved, nor are they necessarily indicative that the doer of these good works has true faith. "It is clear then that to a Christian man his faith suffices for everything, and that he has no need of works for justification. But if he has no need of works, neither has he need of the law; and if he has no need of the law, he is certainly free from the law, and the saying is true, 'The law is not made for a righteous man' (1 Tim. i. 9). This is that Christian liberty, our faith, the effect of which is, not that we should be careless or lead a bad life, but that no one should need the law or works for justification and salvation."[2]

The Bottom Line:

The orthodox doctrine of forgiveness and salvation through belief in Jesus's death and resurrection is today the essence of what it means to be a Christian. But this doctrine does not find unequivocal support in the Christian scriptures. The New Testament does not answer the central question of what we must do to be saved. Is belief enough? Are good works required? Do we also need to be baptized? Do we need to confess our sins and promise to do better? Do we need to do all these things, or only some? If we sin again after being saved, are we lost forever? Far from supporting the orthodox doctrine, the New Testament writings show just as much support for a doctrine which

---

[2] Martin Luther, "The Freedom of a Christian." Online at *http://www.wsu.edu/~dee/REFORM/FREEDOM.HTM*

predestines people to either salvation or damnation, and which applies only to the Jews.

During the early years of the Jesus movement, there were many competing views of what Jesus taught and of what it meant to be a Christian. Throughout the centuries, the view which we now consider "orthodox" succeeded in establishing itself as the official doctrine and branding all other viewpoints as heresies.[3] But the proponents of orthodoxy were not successful in wiping out all traces of the competition. Throughout the New Testament itself, traces of these alternative doctrines abound. These passages speak for themselves. Salvation through belief in the resurrection was by no means a universal view among Jesus's early followers. It was only one view among many. Based on the portrayal of Jesus himself in the gospels, it is highly doubtful that Jesus's own teachings would have received the orthodox stamp of approval.

As we have seen, we cannot turn to the Bible to resolve these doctrinal disputes, because the Bible itself conveys contradictory messages on the core Christian concepts of sin, forgiveness, and salvation. The orthodox doctrine of salvation through belief in Christ's death and resurrection is not supported by the Bible. The entire foundation of modern Christianity thus crumbles to the ground.

---

[3] For a detailed description of this development, see Bart D. Ehrman, *Lost Christianities* (Oxford University Press, 2003).

Chapter 7: Jesus - God or Man?

Orthodox Christian doctrine considers God, Jesus, and the Holy Spirit to be three divine "persons" but comprising only one "god." This is known as the doctrine of the Trinity. If it seems mysterious to you, you are not alone. However, it has become a central tenet of Christianity, and is necessary in order to defend Christianity against charges of polytheism, which both Jews and Muslims level against it. Judaism has only Yahweh, and Islam has only Allah as God. But the Christians have God the father, Jesus his son, the Holy Spirit, the Virgin Mary, plus an assortment of angels and saints, all of whom are immortal and possess various divine traits – not to mention Satan, the god of evil. It is a divine panoply that would stand up proudly against any of the heathen varieties of polytheism, and no doubt this multiplicity of deities helped Christianity seem less foreign to the inhabitants of the Greco-Roman world in which the new religion developed.

It seems odd that the early Christian writers went to such lengths to defend Christianity as a monotheistic religion, instead of just branding it as a new polytheism. Letting go of the monotheistic idea would have allowed the Church to avoid such absurdities as the following: "The Father is God, the Son is God, and the Holy Spirit is God. And yet there are not three Gods, but one God. . . . The Unity is Trinity, and the Trinity is Unity."[1]

---

[1] "The Athanasian Creed," *Catholic Encyclopedia,* online at *http://www.newadvent.org/cathen/02033b.htm.*

Now there's nothing illogical about saying that three separate things form one of some other kind of thing. After all, the motto of the United States is *E Pluribus Unum* – "out of many, one." Thus, fifty states make one nation. Similarly, three gods could make one "Godhead" or perhaps one "divine council." But three gods cannot make one god, any more than three dogs make one dog. The problem comes when the Christians count up the number of gods they have, because they do not want to count them up and say they have three gods. They want to say that God the Father, God the Son, and God the Holy Spirit make one God, at the same time that each one individually is a god. This, of course, does severe violence to the meanings of the concepts "one" and "three." It simply cannot be.

But apart from the murky logic of the Trinity, the doctrine also rests on the idea that Jesus, the Son, is himself a god. Can we find any consistent support for this notion anywhere in the New Testament? As you might expect, the answer is "No." Again we find internal contradictions within the Bible itself, for there are a few verses that explicitly proclaim Jesus as identical or equal with God. But there are many more passages that clearly identify Jesus as being different from God. From a logical standpoint, these two positions contradict each other. But by the preponderance of evidence, the overwhelming picture from the New Testament is that Jesus was at the very least a being distinct from and subordinate to God, and quite possibly not even divine at all. The Church's doctrine of the Trinity is simply an attempt to bring the Biblical message in line with the orthodox doctrine and to reconcile the irreconcilable. The Trinity fails both on logical and on scriptural grounds.

Verses claiming that Jesus and God are equal:
- "I and my Father are one." (John 10:30)
- "In the beginning was the word, and the word was with God, and the word was God . . . and the word was made flesh and dwelt among us." (John 1:1, 14)

Verses showing that God is superior to Jesus and separate from him:
- Jesus admits, "My father is greater than I." (John 14:28)
- "No man has seen God at any time." (John 1:18) Yet crowds of people saw Jesus.
- Jesus was not in existence at the beginning, but was created by God at a specific point in time: "Thou art my son; this day have I begotten thee." (Acts 13:33)
- Jesus asks, "Why do you call me good? There is none good but one. That is God." (Mark 10:18) Also see Luke 18:19; Matthew 19:17.
- Jesus declares that God the father has more knowledge than the Son of God: "But of that day and that hour no man knows, no, not the angels which are in heaven, neither the Son, but the Father." (Mark 13:32)
- On the cross, Jesus felt his separation from God, showing that they are not the same being: "My God, My God, why hast thou forsaken me?" (Mark 15:34) Also Matthew 27:46. (No one can forsake himself, even if he is a god.)
- According to Paul, God the father is superior to Jesus: "The head of every man is Christ; and the head of the woman is the man; and the head of Christ is God." (1 Corinthians 11:3)
- "You are Christ's; and Christ is God's." (1 Corinthians 3:23)
- Paul also identifies Jesus as a descendant of King David "according to the flesh" (Romans 1:3; also see Romans 9:5), which is inconsistent with the notion that he was

divinely conceived by the holy spirit and born of a virgin.
- Peter refers to Jesus the Nazarene as a "man" through whom God performed many wonders. (Acts 2:22) The Greek word used here is *andra*, a form of *aner*, which means "man," but more specifically "a male person of full age and stature, as opposed to a child or female."[2] This usage implies that Jesus was a physical male human being, who did not perform miracles himself, but was the human instrument by which God himself performed these wonders.
- "Among them that are born of women there has not risen a greater than John the Baptist." (Matthew 11:11) But Jesus himself was born of a woman, as we are reminded in Galatians 4:4, so he too was no greater than John the Baptist. But if he was no greater than John the Baptist, how could he possibly have been a god? Therefore, Jesus must not be divine. See also Luke 7:28.
- And in a very odd miracle story, Jesus needs a "do-over" to correct a botched healing of a blind man, showing that he is not perfect and does not possess the omnipotence we would expect of a god. Mark 8:23-25 describes Jesus spitting into the blind man's eyes and laying his hands on him, but when the man looked up, his vision was still impaired, because the people he saw looked like trees walking around. Jesus tried again, and then the man was able to see things clearly. An all-powerful god would have gotten it right the first time.

Based on these verses alone, the biblical evidence is overwhelming that Jesus was not equal to God, but was inferior and subordinate to him. This alone would be a

---

[2] William D. Mounce, *The Analytical Lexicon to the Greek New Testament* (Zondervan, 1993), p.77.

severe blow to the doctrine of the Trinity and to Jesus's divine status. But what about those who were closest to Jesus? Surely his own family and hometown acquaintances would have seen signs of his divinity as they watched him grow up in Nazareth. But in fact, the New Testament paints a very different picture.

A Prophet Without Honor

Given the predictions attendant upon his conception and birth, one would think that those who knew Jesus best would have been his most enthusiastic champions in his role as divine son and world savior. But this is not what we find in the Bible itself. Jesus's own family and townspeople were the most skeptical about his supernatural powers.

Based on the birth narratives of Matthew and Luke, Jesus's acquaintances should have been well aware of the exalted role that he was destined to play. Recall the story of the angel Gabriel who appeared to Mary before she was married to Joseph. Gabriel tells her "Fear not, Mary: for you have found favour with God. And, behold, you shall conceive in your womb, and bring forth a son, and shall call his name Jesus. He shall be great, and shall be called the Son of the Highest: and the Lord God shall give unto him the throne of his father David. And he shall reign over the house of Jacob for ever; and of his kingdom there shall be no end." (Luke 1:30-33) Similarly, Matthew has an angel appearing to Joseph after Mary becomes pregnant, informing him "that which is conceived in her is of the Holy Ghost. And she shall bring forth a son, and you shall call his name Jesus, for he shall save his people from their sins." (Matthew 1:20-21) Wise men came to visit the baby Jesus, calling him "he that is born king of the Jews." (Matthew 2:2). Mary's kinswoman Elizabeth greets Mary as "the mother of my Lord" (Luke 1:43). In the famous Magnificat, Mary rejoices, and brags that "henceforth all generations shall call me blessed." (Luke 1:48) And in Luke's nativity story, the shepherds are told by an angel that "unto you is born this day in the city of David a Saviour, which is Christ the Lord." (Luke 2:11) These shepherds go to visit the baby Jesus, and spread the news given to them by the angel. (Luke 2:16-18)

Given this big buildup, you would think that all throughout Jesus's childhood, his parents, kinsmen, and others living in Nazareth would have kept a close eye on this child, looking for signs of divine wisdom and hints of the great king to be. But in fact, the people closest to Jesus were his greatest scoffers and skeptics. When Jesus begins preaching in his hometown, those who know him are amazed at his new-found fame. Clearly, Jesus's family and the townspeople of Nazareth did not consider him to be divine, despite the greatness that was allegedly prophesied for him by the angels.

Verses showing that Jesus was not accepted as divine by his own family and townspeople:

- While preaching in his hometown, he drew a large crowd, "and when his friends heard of it, they went out to lay hold on him: for they said, He is beside himself." (Mark 3:21)[3]

---

[3] An alternate reading of this verse, supported by both grammar and context, is that Jesus's own family members were the ones saying he was beside himself. See Daniel B. Wallace, *Greek Grammar Beyond the Basics: An Exegetical Syntax of the New Testament,* p.403.

- "Neither did his brothers believe in him." (John 7:5)
- When Jesus taught at the synagogue in his own hometown, the townspeople "were astonished" at his wisdom. So much so that they asked, "Is not this the carpenter's son? Is not his mother called Mary? And his brothers, James, and Joses, and Simon, and Judas? And his sisters, are they not all with us? Whence then has this man all these things? And they were offended at him. But Jesus said unto them, A prophet is not without honour, save in his own country, and in his own house. And he did not [do] many mighty works there because of their unbelief." (Matthew 13:54-58) Notice that the people refer to Jesus as "the carpenter's son" and not as the son of God.
- Mark tells the same story, noting that "he could there do no mighty work, save that he laid his hands upon a few sick folk, and healed them." (Mark 6:5)
- In Luke's account, the people ask, "Is not this Joseph's son?" (Luke 4:22) Again, the townspeople of Nazareth think of Jesus as Joseph's son, not God's son.
- As Jesus continued to preach to the residents of Nazareth, "all they in the synagogue, when they heard these things, were filled with wrath, and rose up, and thrust him out of the city, and led him unto the brow of the hill whereon their city was built, that they might cast him down headlong. But he, passing through the midst of them, went his way." (Luke 4:28-30). Would the townspeople of Nazareth have acted with such disrespect to someone they thought was a god?
And Jesus's own people are not the only ones who chased him out of town. In Mark 5:17 the Gerasenes also asked him to leave their region after he sent the unclean spirits that had possessed a man into a herd of 2000 pigs who then stampeded over a cliff. (Mark does not record whether Jesus reimbursed the owner of the pigs for his loss.)

Now these passages tell us some very interesting things about how Jesus was viewed by his own people. First of all, there is no suggestion that any of them viewed him as anything other than a human being, a man in the flesh, and not as a divine being begotten by the holy spirit. They refer to him as "Joseph's son" or "the carpenter's son" and not as the son of God. He is very much identified with his earthly family, and not with any heavenly ancestry. His earthly family is obviously comprised of individuals of very humble station, which contributes to everyone's astonishment at the wisdom of his teaching. And the fact that he could do no mighty works there indicates that, like any magician, he performed best with a gullible audience. Now there's nothing in these accounts that rules out an ordinary earthly Jesus suddenly becoming inspired by the holy spirit, but this would not be consistent with the birth stories and the fanfare associated with the predictions of the angels, magi, and shepherds. If those closest to Jesus thought of him as just a man, how can we give any credibility to the stories of his divine birth? To the extent that the testimony of the New Testament is reliable at all, it points overwhelmingly to Jesus as being entirely human, and not divine.

But let's look in the other direction and ask how Jesus behaves toward his own family members. Surely he treats his mother Mary with great honor and deference due to her special role as the one chosen by God to bear his son, the savior of mankind. But in fact, Jesus denies his mother no less than Peter denied Jesus himself.

Verses showing Jesus's disrespect for Mary:
- In the Magnificat, Mary rejoiced that "all generations will call me blessed." (Luke 1:48). But her blessedness

did not even extend to the first generation, because it was denied by Jesus himself. We see this in Luke's gospel, where a woman approaches Jesus and exclaims, "Blessed is the womb that bore you, and the breasts that you sucked!" (Luke 11:27) (RSV) But Jesus responds "Rather, blessed are they that hear the word of God and keep it!" (Luke 11:28) The NASB translation brings out the contrast even more, rendering verse 28 as: "On the contrary, blessed are those who hear the word of God, and observe it." Thus, Jesus rejects the woman's blessing of the womb that bore him.

- While Jesus was speaking to the crowds, someone told him his mother and brothers were outside wanting to speak to him. But Jesus answered, "Who is my mother? and who are my brothers? And he stretched forth his hand toward his disciples, and said, Behold my mother and my brothers! For whoever shall do the will of my Father which is in heaven, the same is my brother, and sister, and mother." (Matthew 12:46-50) See also Mark 3:31-35 and Luke 8:20-21. Thus Jesus denies Mary even the humble status of being acknowledged as his own earthly mother.

- And when attending a wedding, Mary informed Jesus that the wine had run out, but he responded to her, "Woman, what have I to do with you? My hour has not yet come." (John 2:3-4) Some translations try to obscure the abrupt tone in which Jesus speaks to his mother by softening the translation. For example, NIV has this as "Dear woman, why do you involve me?" which is highly creative and not at all a literal translation. It turns out that the exact same Greek phrase appears in Mark 5:7 in the mouth of the demon that possessed the man in the land of the Gerasenes. But in this case the NIV translation is coarser: "What do you want with me, Jesus?"

The Bottom Line:

The Bible does not support the doctrine that Jesus is equal to God, or that he is divine at all. There are numerous verses in the New Testament that describe Jesus as a being distinct from and less than God, and a human being at that. Furthermore, according to the gospels themselves, those who were closest to Jesus did not consider him as divine or treat him as such. They display no familiarity at all with the mythical birth stories involving angels and wise men, and predictions of future greatness. Finally, Jesus's treatment of his own mother Mary, shows that he did not treat her with the deference we would expect if she had really been chosen by God to bear his son for the purpose of saving the world from its sins. We are led to the inescapable conclusion that the Bible itself does not support the notion that Jesus was divine. The doctrine of the Trinity thus succumbs to the weight of the Biblical evidence.

Chapter 8: The End Was Near

There is a grand climax that Christianity builds to. It is variously known as the kingdom of God, the day of judgment, the second coming, the end times, or the eschaton. It is the day when God's power and authority over the world will become obvious to all. At that time God will triumph once and for all over the forces of evil. God and/or Jesus Christ will judge the living and the dead, and hold everyone accountable for their deeds, good and bad. The gospels describe various signs that will accompany these last days. But when will these events occur?

The answer given throughout the New Testament is that they will come soon, but we can be more specific than that. The end of time was to occur *during the lifetime of those to whom Jesus was speaking.* (In case you didn't notice, it never happened.)

In the Gospel of Mark, Jesus tells the crowds: "Whoever therefore shall be ashamed of me and of my words in this adulterous and sinful generation; of him also shall the Son of man be ashamed, when he comes in the glory of his Father with the holy angels. And he said unto them, Verily I say unto you, That there be some of them that stand here, which shall not taste of death, till they have seen the kingdom of God come with power." (Mark 8:38-9:1)

In chapter 13 of Mark's gospel, Jesus tells us in some detail what to expect: "But in those days, after that tribulation, the sun shall be darkened, and the moon shall not give her light. And the stars of heaven shall fall, and the powers that are in heaven shall be shaken. And then shall they see the Son of man coming in the clouds with great power and glory. And then shall he send his angels, and shall gather together his elect from the four winds, from the uttermost part of the earth to the uttermost part of heaven. Now learn a parable of the fig tree: When her branch is yet tender, and puts forth leaves, you know that summer is near: So you in like manner, when you shall see these things come to pass, know that it is near, even at the doors. Verily I say unto you, that *this generation shall not pass, till all these things be done."* (Mark 13:24-30)

I've quoted this entire passage to show that nothing is taken out of context here. Certainly the signs that Jesus foretells would be hard to miss. He is not talking about events that are vague or subtle. These signs would be obvious and would command the attention of anyone living at the time. But the detail of greatest interest to us is when this calamity will take place: "*This generation* shall not pass till *all* these things be done." In other words, *all* of these spectacular events would take place, and some of the very individuals that were alive when Jesus was speaking would still be alive to see them all occur.

The Greek word for generation, *genea*, means essentially the same as our English word, so trying to stretch the meaning to include the entire "generation" of mankind does not escape the difficulty. The editors of the Oxford Annotated Bible tell us that "the normal meaning of *this generation* would be 'men of our time,' and the words would refer to a period of 20-30 years. What Jesus meant, however, is uncertain"[1] But it is only uncertain to those who refuse to accept the possibility that Jesus could be wrong. You cannot make him right without inventing new definitions for the words in the text.

---

[1] *The New Oxford Annotated Bible,* p.1204.

Christian apologists often appeal to Mark 13:32 to argue that Jesus was not making a specific prediction about when the end would occur. That passage tells us that Jesus himself does not know exactly when the end will come: "But of that day and that hour knoweth no man, no, not the angels which are in heaven, neither the Son, but the Father." (Mark 13:32) Here, however, he's just telling us that he doesn't know the *exact* time when the kingdom of God will arrive. He is still very clear that it will occur sometime during the lifetime of the generation he's speaking to, which, as we've seen, could give a range of approximately 20-30 years, or certainly no more than a normal human lifespan. In any case, the Christians might not want to call too much attention to Mark 13:32, because it raises additional difficulties for them. For one, it shows that Jesus is not omniscient (i.e., doesn't know everything), which undermines his status as a *bona fide* deity. And since God the Father *does* know when the end will come, this verse contradicts the notion that Jesus and God are one. The plain meaning of Mark 13:32 is that Jesus is different from, and inferior to, God the Father, but it does not overturn Jesus's prediction that the end would come within the lifetimes of his listeners.

These verses from Mark's Gospel are not isolated instances. In Matthew we see the same message of the judgment day coming in the very near future. He tells the disciples that their mission is to "Go not into the way of the Gentiles, and into any city of the Samaritans enter ye not. But go rather to the lost sheep of the house of Israel. And as you go, preach, saying, The kingdom of heaven is at hand. . . . *You shall not have gone over the cities of Israel, till the Son of man has come.*" (Matthew 10:5-7, 23) And again, "Verily I say unto you: There are some standing here, who *shall not taste of death, till they see the Son of man coming in his kingdom.* (Matthew 16:28) This last verse is even more specific than "this generation" in declaring that some of those who are "standing here" will still be alive when the kingdom arrives.

In the 24th chapter of Matthew, the disciples ask Jesus, "When shall these things be? And what shall be the sign of your coming, and of the end of the world?" (Matthew 24:3) Jesus answers them with a very detailed description of the end times which closely parallels that of Mark 13: "The sun [shall] be darkened, and the moon shall not give her light, and the stars shall fall from heaven, and the powers of the heavens shall be shaken: And then shall appear the sign of the Son of man in heaven: and then shall all the tribes of the earth mourn, and they shall see the Son of man coming in the clouds of heaven with power and great glory. And he shall send his angels with a great sound of a trumpet, and they shall gather together his elect from the four winds, from one end of heaven to the other." (Matthew 24:29-31) Again, these are not the sort of events that might have escaped the notice of those who were living at the time. But when was all this supposed to happen? "Verily I say unto you, *this generation shall not pass*, till *all* these things be fulfilled." (Matthew 24:34) As we saw above, the Greek word for generation means basically the same as our word, and would normally imply a time period of 20-30 years, or certainly no longer than a normal human lifespan. Once again, Jesus's prediction was wrong.

And there's more: The gospel of Luke has a passage nearly identical to the one at the end of Mark's chapter 8: "For whoever shall be ashamed of me and of my words, of him shall the Son of man be ashamed, when he shall come in his own glory, and in his Father's, and of the holy angels.

But I tell you of a truth, there be some standing here, which *shall not taste of death*, till they see the kingdom of God.." (Luke 9:26-27) There is no escape by claiming that "taste of death" has some metaphorical or symbolic meaning. The Oxford Annotated Bible has a footnote here to confirm that "taste death" means "to die." Note that this same expression is used to mean "die" in John 8:52 and in Hebrews 2:9. Luke is only slightly less dramatic than Mark and Matthew in describing the arrival of the kingdom: "And there shall be signs in the sun, and in the moon, and in the stars; and upon the earth distress of nations, with perplexity; the sea and the waves roaring; Men's hearts failing them for fear, and for looking after those things which are coming on the earth. For the powers of heaven shall be shaken. And then shall they see the Son of man coming in a cloud with power and great glory. . . Verily I say unto you, *This generation shall not pass away, till all be fulfilled.*" (Luke 21:25-27, 32)

One commonly attempted escape from the dilemma created by Mark 13:30, Matthew 24:34 and Luke 21:32 is to claim that the generation referred to is not the generation Jesus is speaking to, but the generation that will be living at the time these amazing events take place. But this is obviously absurd, because it would mean that Jesus is telling his audience, "Some of the people in the generation that will be alive when these things happen will be alive when these things happen." A statement like this conveys no meaning at all, and there would be no point in Jesus saying it. Also, this attempted defense ignores the usual meaning of the word "this." "This" generation, like "this" pencil or "this" apple, means the one closest to the speaker. If we're talking about something far away, we use "that." If Jesus were really talking about the generation that will be living at some future time, he would not have said "this" generation. Instead, he would have said "that" generation. The distinction is the same in Greek as in English.

We see the same theme throughout the other books of the New Testament. They all consider the end to be near - very near. And believers should not immerse themselves in the cares of the world, but should prepare themselves for the end which is fast approaching:

- "Now it is high time to awake out of sleep: for now is our salvation nearer than when we believed. The night is far spent, the day is at hand." (Romans 13:11-12)
- The sins of ancient Israel were written down "for our admonition, upon whom the ends of the world have come." (1 Corinthians 10:11)
- "The time is short," says Paul in 1 Corinthians 7:29. Consequently, he advises that "they that have wives be as though they had none." Here Paul is advising the married believers to live as though they were celibate, for the end is so close that one mustn't allow oneself to be distracted with earthly pleasures.
- "We who are alive, who are left until the coming of the Lord, shall not precede those who have fallen asleep." (1 Thessalonians 4:15) (RSV) "Fall asleep" is a euphemism frequently used by Paul to mean "die." Here he is assuring his readers that those believers who are still alive for Jesus's return will not take precedence in heaven over those who have already died. Obviously, Paul expects that some of his fellow believers will still be alive when Jesus returns. Some Christians try to interpret "we" in this passage to mean Christians in general, rather than Paul and his followers. This would allow the passage to mean that "some Christians" will still be living when Jesus returns, but not necessarily Paul or any of his followers. There is no basis for this interpretation in the text, and no reason to think that Paul is using "we" in any but the normal sense."

- "The coming of the Lord draws nigh." (James 5:8)
- "The time is at hand." (Revelation 1:3; 22:10)
- "Behold, I come quickly." (Revelation 3:11; 22:12)

What makes this such a damaging issue for the Christians is that Jesus is shown to be wrong about a prediction that marks the culmination of the entire Christian narrative. It raises serious doubt as to his status as the son of God and as the savior of mankind. It lends strong support to the position of the Jews and Muslims, who have always rejected the idea that Jesus of Nazareth was a divine messiah. And it is not just an isolated passage that reveals to us this failed prediction. This same prediction is repeated again and again, in very specific terms, from multiple authors and in various expressions. All three of the synoptic gospels agree in predicting that Jesus would return after his death to establish the kingdom of God and that this would occur within the lifetime of those who were listening to his words. This return would be accompanied by various astronomical marvels such as the world had never seen, with Jesus himself riding down from the sky on clouds of glory. Jesus gambled all his chips on this prediction – and lost.

> "When a prophet speaks in the name of the LORD, if the word does not come to pass or come true, that is a word which the LORD has not spoken; the prophet has spoken it presumptuously, you need not be afraid of him." (Deuteronomy 18:22) (RSV)

As you might imagine, the Christian apologists cannot let this theological disaster go without an attempt to salvage the situation. But their defensive options are limited. The plain reading of the gospels is devastating, so their only hope is to reinterpret the Bible's words to mean something other than what they actually say. For example, it can be claimed that Jesus's use of time was symbolic rather than literal. We see an example of this argument in the book of 2 Peter. Remember that the books of the New Testament were written over a period of several decades, some perhaps as much as a hundred years after Jesus himself lived and preached. By that time, many believers in the Jesus movement were beginning to wonder whether he would ever come back, given the high expectation of an early return. The author of 2 Peter notes the presence of "scoffers" in the last days, who ask "Where is the promise of his coming?" (2 Peter 3:4) The author of the letter responds by pointing out that "one day is with the Lord as a thousand years, and a thousand years as one day." (2 Peter 3:8) But this retort misses the point. Jesus did not set the time of his return as a certain number of days or years. He said it would be within the lifetime of those listening to him. So whatever unit of time God was following, things would still need to be wrapped up before all of those first generation Christians had passed away. Thus, the reliance on a different standard of heavenly time does not remove the contradiction between Jesus's prediction and historical reality.

The author of 2 Peter goes on to say that another reason for God's delay is his desire to give more people a chance to repent of their sins. (2 Peter 3:9) The problem with this is that while a few of these tardy sinners are finally coming around to repent, millions of new sinners have been born who have not yet repented and who never will. On balance, in the nearly 2000 years since the Christian era began, the wait has resulted in a net increase of several billion non-

Christian unrepentant sinners in the world – more fuel for the fires of hell. So it cannot be argued that the long delay in the arrival of the end times is an act of mercy on the part of God, who is giving us all extra time to be saved.

Another attempted defense from the Christians is to allege that the "kingdom of God" is to be understood in non-apocalyptic terms, and interpret it in such a way that it could have already happened. Those who take this approach consider the kingdom of God to refer to the establishment and growth of the Christian church, and the spread of the gospel message to all nations of the earth. Now the Christian church did in fact become established and grow, and the message of Christianity has for all practical purposes been preached in all the world. But this interpretation ignores the very specific astronomical signs described by Jesus. He simply has not arrived from heaven on clouds of glory, and the sun and moon have not lost their light, and the stars have not fallen down from heaven as was expected. There's no doubt that whatever Jesus was predicting, it was going to be a spectacular show, and no one would miss it. The claim that he was referring to the establishment and growth of the Catholic Church is anticlimactic in the extreme and simply does not fit with his own reported words.

Finally, there have been attempts to identify the events predicted by Jesus with the fall of Jerusalem in 70 AD in the Jewish revolt against the Romans. But this argument has even been rejected by such Christian apologists as A. L. Moore in his book on the second coming. Moore tells us that such passages as Mark 9:1 "can hardly be taken as a prediction of the fall of Jerusalem. . . . Chiefly because a) the downfall of Jerusalem is never spoken of as the 'coming of the Kingdom of God' . . . and b) other references to 'the coming of the Kingdom' cannot support such an identification."[2]

Moore, by the way, reaches a conclusion similar to that expressed in 2 Peter 3:9, i.e., that God is giving us a grace period in which to repent, while the end has remained "near" throughout all these two thousand years. His conclusion depends heavily on interpretations that go far beyond the plain meaning of the language in the New Testament. And again, many more sinners have been born since Jesus lived, so God would have done better to cut his losses and send judgment when Jesus predicted instead of waiting while the world added a few billion more unrepentant sinners. Besides, if God were going to give us this extra time, wouldn't Jesus have known about it beforehand and figured it into his prediction?

But perhaps the best way to counter these types of arguments is to again invoke the 2nd Peter principle, which tells us that nothing in the scripture is a matter of one's own individual interpretation. (2 Peter 1:20) Either the Christians must accept the Bible for what it says, with all its contradictions, or they must reinterpret it to make it internally and externally consistent. But such reinterpretation is forbidden by 2 Peter 1:20. The Christians are caught between the rock of contradiction and the hard place of disobedience.

---

[2] A.L. Moore, *The Parousia in the New Testament: Supplements to Novum Testamentum, vol. XIII* (E.J. Brill, 1966), p.104.

Chapter 9: Paul Against Himself

We've seen that the New Testament is awash with internal contradictions. We've also seen that these contradictions are not limited to matters of mere detail, but strike to the heart of Christian doctrine. But might it be possible for a Christian to carve out some kind of coherent religious doctrine by limiting their focus to just one author out of all the 27 books of the New Testament? Many Christians would say yes, it is possible. And the author they would point to is Paul.

We have already noted that many scholars consider Paul to be the true founder of Christianity. Paul's letters are the earliest surviving records dealing with the issue of sin and salvation, and the central role of Jesus Christ in leading sinners from the one to the other. The character of Christianity as we know it today is heavily dependent on Paul's development of these themes, both in his letters and in his missionary work with several early Christian communities outside the Jewish homeland. Even though the other New Testament authors may not always agree with him, surely the man who established Christianity as a separate religion distinct from Judaism will paint us a consistent picture of what Christianity is all about, right?

By now it will come as no surprise that the answer is no. We shall see that Paul himself presents no clear and unified set of beliefs that we can identify as the essence of Christianity. Since Paul's writings are the most complete and comprehensive of any in the New Testament in terms of theological development, this last redoubt of the Christians falls. Having exposed the myth of biblical infallibility, and revealed the central Christian doctrines to be riddled with inconsistencies, we now show that the very architect of Christian theology reverses and contradicts himself again and again, and that his theological system, even in its most basic form, stumbles over its own logic as soon as it leaves the starting block.

Raymond Brown, in his widely praised *Introduction to the New Testament*, finds that Paul's theology is such a large subject that "even a sketch" is beyond the scope of his 800-page book.[1] He notes that many books have been devoted to the elucidation of Paul's theological position, which a perusal of Brown's very thorough bibliography confirms. If we recall that Paul's entire literary output consists of the letters contained in the New Testament, and that only seven of those are indisputably his, then it is astounding that such a small body of work should require such an ocean of explanatory material. The genuine letters of Paul comprise about 32,000 words, and even with the disputed letters the total only comes to around 42,000 words. (That's shorter than the book you're reading.) If Paul had written clearly and consistently, there would be no need for so much commentary. The only reason that Paul's theology is deemed to be complex is that it requires a great deal of linguistic and philosophic sleight of hand to pull a consistent story out of the mishmash. As Brown notes, "scholars are far from agreement on the key issue in Paul's thought."[2] This is an astounding admission about the foundations of the Christian faith. Not only is there disagreement over Paul's meaning, but there is not even any consensus on what the *key issue* is in his writings. If Paul is

---

[1] Raymond E. Brown, *An Introduction to the New Testament* (Doubleday, 1997), p.437.
[2] Ibid., p.440.

not comprehensible, then Christianity itself is not comprehensible.

For those of us who take Paul at face value, his theology is easy to explain: Here he says one thing, there he says the opposite. In another place he constructs an argument that self-destructs because of simple logical fallacies. It's easy to understand his message. It's just not easy to make it coherent. Unless you are desperate to preserve the illusion of biblical infallibility, there is no need for such a gargantuan effort to fit the square peg of Paul into the round hole of reason. (Paul, obsessed as he was about such things, would no doubt find something decidedly naughty in such a metaphor.)

Paul's Theology

When Paul was writing, there were no written gospels in existence. The gospels of Matthew, Mark, Luke, and John would not be written for another decade or more. Paul wrote during a time when there was much confusion and disappointment among Jesus's followers over his crucifixion. If Jesus was the promised messiah, the warrior king predicted by the Hebrew scriptures, why was he captured and killed? The movement would not survive unless some plausible meaning could be found for the glaring failure of Jesus's earthly mission. This is what Paul's theology provides. By giving a purpose to Jesus's death, Paul gave the movement new life. In his view, Jesus was a sacrifice for the sins of mankind. Just as the Jews sacrificed animals to placate Yahweh for violating Yahweh's laws, there also needed to be a sacrifice to atone for all the sins of mankind. "For the wages of sin is death."

(Romans 6:23) And the only way to escape death is to offer an appropriate sacrifice. But what sacrifice would be great enough to atone for all the sins of mankind? Only one who is without sin could be pure enough to balance out so much human wickedness. Jesus, being the son of God and without sin, was the only possible offering for such a sacrifice.

Paul's most comprehensive attempt at systematic theology is presented in his letter to the Romans. It is this letter that gives him the reputation of being a profound theological thinker. But obscurity does not necessarily imply profundity. When we analyze Paul's presentation of the orthodox Christian doctrine in Romans and in his other letters, we find that it quickly falls apart.

Original sin

Whereas the Greeks revered the beauty of the human body and its likeness to the gods, the foundation of Paul's theology is sin – especially the sinful nature of bodily flesh. According to Romans 3:23, all have sinned, and we read in Romans 5:12 that the sin which is inherent in humankind is traced all the way back to Adam, the first human created by God: "Therefore just as through one man sin came into the world, and death through sin, so also death spread to all men because they all sinned." For Paul, there is no doubt about where this sinful nature resides. It is in the flesh. "The mind that is set on the flesh is hostile toward God." (Romans 8:7) (RSV) "If you live according to the flesh you will die." (Romans 8:13)

Right away here we have a problem, and not just one problem. First of all, the doctrine of original sin depends entirely on the historical truth of the story of Adam. Any

Christian who believes that the temptation of Adam and Eve in the Garden of Eden is just an allegory or myth, unwittingly undermines their belief in the Christian doctrine of salvation, for without original sin, the need for salvation disappears. No wonder the fundamentalists fight so hard to keep the teaching of evolution out of the public schools.

But even if, for the sake of argument, we accept the Adam story as true, Paul is still in deep trouble, because he is saying two different things in Romans 5:12. On the one hand, he tells us that sin and death have spread to all men through one man, that is, Adam. But he finishes the thought by saying that "death spread to all men, *because they all sinned.*" So, did sin and death spread because Adam's sin extended to all, or because "they all sinned"? In other words, are we sinful because of the sinful nature we inherited from Adam, or because we ourselves, every one of us, have committed sinful acts? Paul is not clear on this, and by reading further in his letters we do not get any clarification. It is critically important to his doctrine that the principle of original sin inherited through Adam be upheld, for it is essential to his concept of salvation. This becomes vividly obvious when we read Romans 5:19: "For as by one man's disobedience many were made sinners, so by the obedience of one shall many be made righteous."

Thus, if sin were not inherited, and if it resulted simply from the particular sinful acts of each individual, the argument for Jesus's sacrifice would not work. There would be different degrees of sin in different sinners. Since a newborn baby cannot sin, there would be people who are totally innocent until they commit their first sin. Some might take a long time before committing that first sin, and might even die before they do so. In that case, there would be no basis for inflicting any punishment whatsoever upon them and no need for any atonement or salvation. So Paul and the orthodox doctrine need the concept of original sin, as inherited by all humankind from Adam, the original sinner, in order to justify their notion that we all need to be saved.

Paul's argument is that the original sin which entered mankind through one man, and condemned us all to death, was balanced out by the sacrifice of one perfect man, the sinless Jesus, who gave hope of eternal life. The judgment of the many arose from the sin of one man. And the possibility of eternal life for the many arose from the sacrifice of another man. Of course, it is only an argument by analogy, not a real proof, but given the standards of the times, it appears to have satisfied many, at least among the common people. Paul met with a rather more skeptical audience when he tried to explain his system to the Greek philosophers in Athens. (Acts 17:18)

But Paul's scheme becomes murkier as we look more closely into it. Note that it depends on three key points:

1) Original sin affecting all people;
2) Jesus as the totally innocent and sinless sacrificial victim;
3) The parallel between Jesus's act of sacrifice and the sacrifices required under the Jewish law.

We have already seen that the first key concept – original sin – is doubtful because Paul is not clear whether we inherit sin from Adam, or if all humans commit sin on their own. But what about the second point? Paul had never met Jesus, so could not know from personal experience whether he was a sinner or not, and he had no gospels to refer to. But we do have the gospels and it's legitimate for us to ask: Was Jesus really the totally innocent lamb required by Paul's theological argument?

The Sins of Jesus

Jesus as the innocent sacrificial victim is a critical feature of Paul's theological argument. If Jesus was a sinner, then he is just as much in need of a savior as the rest of us. Paul's argument only makes sense if the one being sacrificed on behalf of humankind is himself totally blameless. The Old Testament makes it clear that Yahweh is not pleased with a defective sacrifice: "You shall not sacrifice unto the LORD thy God any bullock, or sheep, wherein is blemish, or any evilfavouredness: for that is an abomination unto the LORD thy God." (Deuteronomy 17:1) So if Jesus is going to step into the role of sacrificial lamb, he has to be perfect and totally free of sin – i.e., unblemished, as God's law requires for all sacrifices. Paul's assumption that Jesus is such an unblemished sacrifice is set forth in 2 Corinthians 5:21. "He has made him to be sin for us, who knew no sin." Although the book of Hebrews was not written by Paul, the same idea is expressed there, as Jesus is described as "holy, blameless, unstained." (Hebrews 7:26) (RSV)

The idea of Jesus as a sinner will strike many Christians as absurd, but only because they haven't looked into the matter. However, if the innocence of Jesus is a premise of Paul's argument, we are justified in testing that premise to see if it is true. We cannot simply assume that Jesus was sinless; we have to check it out. Let's start by looking at what Paul considered to be a sin, and then we'll compare

Jesus's actions from the gospels to see if he committed any of them.

Paul is very clear that sin comes from the Law. "Without the law, sin was dead." (Romans 7:8) "The law is holy, and the commandment holy and just and good." (Romans 7:12) In Paul's earlier letter to the Galatians, we read "For I testify again to every man that is circumcised, that he is a debtor to do the whole law." (Galatians 5:3) Thus, the law is an obligation to every man who is circumcised.[3] Now, if we take the gospels as our only evidence of Jesus's life, we know that Jesus received circumcision, because Luke tells us so in Luke 2:21. Therefore, by Paul's own reckoning, Jesus is obligated to keep the whole Jewish Law. It's true that Paul also says repeatedly that Christians are no longer under the obligation of the Law (for example, Romans 7:4-6), but that is because they have died to the Law in Jesus's crucifixion. Jesus, as a living Jewish man before the crucifixion, would not qualify for this exemption from the Law. Therefore, we should expect to see, in the gospels, that Jesus at all times followed the Law, if he was indeed sinless and perfect.

But what exactly is "following the Law"? In the very broadest sense, it means keeping God's commandments, and for observant Jews it specifically means the commandments laid down in the Torah, the first five books of the Old Testament attributed to Moses. Paul tries to sum it up by saying that all the commandments are satisfied if you "love your neighbor as yourself." For Paul, "love is the fulfilling of the law." (Romans 13:9-10) It so happens that this position undermines Paul's doctrine on original sin,

---

[3] Paul does not say whether women have any obligation to obey the law, or only to obey their husbands, as he (or someone writing in his name) teaches in Ephesians 5:22 and Colossians 3:18.

because if loving one's neighbor is all that is required to avoid sin, then there are undoubtedly many individuals who would qualify as free of sin.

But there is no basis in the scriptures for collapsing all the Law into this one commandment, and a practicing Jew in Jesus's lifetime would not have taken this position. Many of the commandments in the Old Testament specifically state that they are to apply as "perpetual statutes," and thus no relaxation of their requirements was allowed. And indeed Jesus himself declared that not a single letter of the law would pass away until all has been fulfilled. (Matthew 5:18) Granted, Jesus contradicts himself on this later on, where he himself collapses the whole Law down to two commandments in Matthew 22:37-40. But if we are testing to see whether Jesus himself sinned or not, we cannot very well let him choose which commandments must be followed. So we will take the position that Jesus, as a practicing Jew, was obligated by Jewish law to follow the commandments of God as laid down in the Torah. Violation of any of these commandments would constitute a sin on Jesus's part.

There are many commandments, some weighty, some trivial all through the books of the Torah, but starting with the ten commandments, can we find any that Jesus violated? Even if he violated only one of them, that makes Jesus a sinner, and unqualified to play the role of the perfectly innocent victim who is sacrificed for the sins of humankind. As a reminder, here are the ten commandments as summarized from Exodus 20:2-17:

1. You shall have no other gods before me.
2. You shall not make for yourself a graven image, or any likeness of anything that is in heaven above or that is in the earth beneath, or that is in the water under the earth.

3. You shall not take the name of the LORD your God in vain.
4. Remember the sabbath day, to keep it holy. On the sabbath day you shall not do any work.
5. Honor your father and your mother.
6. You shall not kill.
7. You shall not commit adultery.
8. You shall not steal.
9. You shall not bear false witness against your neighbor.
10. You shall not covet your neighbor's house, wife, manservant, maidservant, ox, donkey, or anything else belonging to your neighbor. ("Covet" means to desire or wish for.)

Right away we see that there are several of these commandments that Jesus broke. Yahweh commands that we honor our father and mother, but Jesus spoke very harshly to his mother in John 2:4 ("Woman, what have I to do with you?"). He effectively disowned her in public in Matthew 12:46-50, preferring his followers over her. And when the woman in Luke proclaims Mary's womb as "blessed" for having given birth to Jesus, he again objects, and gives preference to those who follow his version of God's word. (Luke 11:27-28) On all these counts, Jesus dishonored his mother, and violated the fifth commandment. Thus, Jesus is a sinner.

Jesus committed a second violation when he commanded his disciples to go into a neighboring village, where they would find a donkey and a colt tied up, and to untie the animals and bring them to him. (Matthew 21:2) Matthew's account does not tell us that they asked anyone for permission to take the donkey and colt, or if they did ask, what the response was. In any case, at least the tenth commandment is violated, because Jesus coveted another person's donkey (and colt). If he had them taken without permission, then he also violated the eighth commandment against stealing. Either way, Jesus violated at least one of God's commandments, and thus sinned against God.

The list of commandments in Exodus does not include a commandment to love God, but we find this elsewhere in the Torah, in Deuteronomy 6:5 – "You shall love the LORD your God with all your heart, and with all your soul, and with all your might." Did Jesus follow this commandment? Not always. We only have to look at Mark's gospel to find an instance where Jesus was expressing anything but love for God. When Jesus cried out on the cross, "My God, my God, why have you forsaken me?" he was certainly not loving God with all his heart, and with all his soul, and with all his might. At least some portion of his heart, soul, and might was expressing disappointment and frustration with God for deserting him just at the moment when Jesus was counting on him to provide support for his movement against the Romans. So again, Jesus violated a commandment of God, and therefore was a sinner.

Jesus is accused repeatedly by the Pharisees of violating the law against doing work on the Sabbath, as expressed not only in the fourth commandment, but also in Exodus 31:15-16 – "Whoever does any work on the sabbath day, he shall surely be put to death. Wherefore the children of Israel shall keep the sabbath, to observe the sabbath throughout their generations, for a *perpetual* covenant." (Emphasis added.) The accusations of violating the Sabbath arise from Jesus's healing of the sick and picking grain on the Sabbath. In chapter 9 of John's gospel, Jesus mixes up a batch of clay on the Sabbath and places it on the eyes of a blind man in order to cure his blindness. Even if merely commanding the sick to be healed could be exempted as not really being work, surely mixing up clay would count as "work" under the law of the Sabbath. Clearly Jesus was not making it a day of complete rest as the commandment requires. The Pharisees, who were the experts on such things, certainly thought so. There is no indication of why Jesus could not wait till the next day to heal the blind man, or heal him without working up a batch of clay. So by working on the Sabbath, Jesus again violated one of God's commandments. The author of John admits as much in John 5:18 where he notes that the Jews were seeking to kill Jesus "because he not only had broken the sabbath, but said also that God was his Father, making himself equal with God." John does not qualify his remarks by saying that the Jews *alleged* these things, but states them as fact. By breaking the Sabbath, Jesus committed a sin.

But we're not done yet with listing the sins of Jesus. Leviticus 5:1 requires that a witness who is summoned in a public proceeding must testify to what he knows. "If any one sins in that he hears a public adjuration to testify and though he is a witness, whether he has seen or come to know the matter, yet does not speak, he shall bear his iniquity." (RSV) However, Jesus, before the Sanhedrin and before Pilate, refused to testify. (Matthew 27:13-14) Thus, by refusing to testify, Jesus violated this commandment as well, which constitutes yet another sin.

"You shall fear the LORD your God, and serve him, and shall swear by his name." (Deuteronomy 6:13) But Jesus counsels his followers to ignore this commandment to swear by Yahweh's name, and tells them instead, "Swear not at all; neither by heaven; for it is God's throne: Nor by the earth; for it is his footstool: neither by Jerusalem; for it is the city of the great King." (Matthew 5:34-35) So not only does Jesus himself break God's commandments, he advises others to do so as well.

In Matthew 23:17, Jesus even broke his own rule by calling the scribes and Pharisees "fools," even though anyone who does so, by his own admission in Matthew 5:22, "shall be in danger of hell fire."

And if Jesus was not a sinner, why did he have to be baptized by John the Baptist? John baptized Jesus in the Jordan river (Mark 1:9; Matthew 3:13-16), and John was preaching a "baptism of repentance for the remission of sins." (Mark 1:4; see also Matthew 3:6.) If Jesus was sinless, then his baptism by John makes no sense. This is not a newly discovered problem: "The Christians of Matthew's time wondered why Jesus, whom they believed to be sinless, had submitted to a baptism which presupposed repentance."[4] "Because John's baptism involves the confession of sins (3:6), Jesus' submission to it is awkward."[5] Matthew's attempt to explain away the awkwardness goes nowhere. He simply has Jesus tell John to let it be for now, as it is appropriate to "fulfill all righteousness." (3:15) But what could possibly be righteous about a sinless man being baptized for sins? And what would the meaning of baptism even be for a man who had not sinned? Jesus came to John specifically for the purpose of being baptized by him (3:13), and there is no satisfactory explanation for this other than that Jesus was a sinner.

We could multiply the examples, but the point has been made. Paul's scheme of salvation depends on a totally innocent and sinless Jesus. But the Jesus of the gospels does not come close to fulfilling this role. According to the

---

[4] *The Interpreter's Bible,* vol. 7, p.267.
[5] John Barton and John Muddiman (eds.), *The Oxford Bible Commentary* (Oxford University Press, 2001), p.851.

gospels, he sinned on numerous occasions by violating laws and commandments laid down in the ancient Hebrew scriptures, which all Jews were obligated to follow. Paul's theology fails because there is no sacrificial person who meets the required standard of perfection.

False Parallels Between Jesus and The Old Testament Sacrifices

Even if Jesus were free of sin, and qualified to make a sacrifice on behalf of all mankind, Paul's theology would still fail, because there are logical holes in the analogy between Adam's sin and Jesus's sacrifice. Paul would have us believe that Adam's sin made sinners of us all, regardless of what we ourselves do, and regardless of whether we accept responsibility for Adam's actions. There is no opt-out clause when it comes to inheriting Adam's original sin. But on the other side he requires an opt-in before Jesus's sacrifice takes effect for any given individual. If indeed Jesus's death atoned for the sins of mankind in the same way that Adam's sin brought death to mankind, there would be no need for each individual to take further action to accept the sacrifice by declaring belief in Jesus's role. Yet this is what Paul requires: "If you will confess with your mouth the Lord Jesus, and will believe in your heart that God has raised him from the dead, you shall be saved." (Romans 10:9)

If we have to make a choice as to whether to accept Jesus's act of sacrifice and salvation, then shouldn't we also have a choice as to whether to accept responsibility for Adam's sinfulness? Paul even admits as much in his earlier letter to the Corinthians, when he says "For as in Adam all die, even so in Christ shall all be made alive."

(1 Corinthians 15:22) According to this passage, not just the believers, but *all* will be made alive by virtue of Christ's sacrifice. And again, "as one man's trespass led to condemnation for all men, so one man's act of righteousness leads to acquittal and life for *all* men." (Romans 5:18) (RSV) Nothing here about having to believe or declare anything. It is the obedience of Christ himself that brings about the salvation for the many. The orthodox Christian doctrine requires an active belief and acceptance of Jesus's sacrifice as a condition for salvation. But here we see that even within Paul's own writings, where this doctrine first finds written expression, we find an opposing viewpoint. From its very beginnings, Christianity was inconsistent in its basic principles.

And yet Paul also says that we are not even free to decide for ourselves whether to believe in and accept Jesus's sacrifice. Who is saved and who is lost has been decided well in advance. And as individuals, we have no control over the power of sin within us. These ideas go against the popular view of Christian salvation, but they are clearly articulated in Paul's letters, where we find that salvation does not depend upon the individual person's will or effort, but on "God who shows mercy." (Romans 9:16) And God has mercy on those he wishes to save, but then hardens the hearts of those poor unfortunates who are not favored with his mercy. (Romans 9:18). Paul goes on to tell the parable of the potter who prepares certain vessels for the sake of beauty, and others for common use and destruction. (Romans 9:21-23) It is entirely up to the whim of the potter as to which ones will be destroyed – the pots have no say in the matter. Salvation then is through God's grace, and he has already chosen in advance those who are to be saved. This dismal outlook flatly contradicts Paul's more hopeful message in Romans 10:9, which promises salvation to anyone who confesses his belief in Jesus and his resurrection. Obviously, Paul did not resolve the theological debate within his own mind before committing his ideas to paper.

There is one more logical difficulty we will consider before leaving the topic of Paul's salvation plan. Romans 8:3 makes it clear that Jesus's sacrifice is an offering for sin, which parallels the Old Testament sin offerings to Yahweh. But the animals sacrificed in the ancient Hebrew rituals stayed dead. There is no record that the rams, bulls, and goats slain as a sin offering ever rose up again after three days and ascended into heaven. If sin brings death – permanent death – and if a sacrifice is really required to compensate for the sins of mankind, then the sacrifice should entail the death – permanent death – of the one sacrificed. How can one day and two nights in a stone tomb balance out the sin and ensuing death of all the human beings that have ever lived or will live upon the earth? If Jesus is spending eternity in heaven at the right hand of God, how can it be said that he has taken on the punishment for the sins of the world, when "the wages of sin is death"? Jesus's "sacrifice" is a bogus one because it was not permanent. There have been many real non-divine humans who have endured more suffering than Jesus did in his few hours on the cross. And it's even questionable whether Jesus suffered at all, because Paul tells us that God sent Jesus his son "in the *likeness* of sinful flesh" as a sacrifice for sin. (Romans 8:3) Thus according to this statement of Paul, Jesus only *appeared* to be fleshly. But if he was not really a physical human body, he could not suffer. If he could not suffer, then there is no sacrifice at all.

It would be easy to fill an entire book with the conflicting theological messages contained in Paul's letters. But these examples will suffice, and the believers who are searching for a kernel of consistency somewhere in the New Testament will not find it in Paul. Given all these contradictions and inconsistencies, what are we to make of Paul's theology? Does it provide a philosophical justification of the Christian scheme of salvation through Jesus Christ? The answer is obviously no. Paul's own words hit the mark when he says, "Unless you utter by the tongue words easy to be understood, how shall it be known what is spoken? For you shall speak into the air." (1 Corinthians 14:9) Perhaps we can only throw up our hands and proclaim as Paul did about God himself, "How unsearchable are his judgments and unfathomable his ways!" (Romans 11:33) (RSV)

Chapter 10: Phony Prophecies from the Old Testament

Old Testament "prophecies" about Jesus are the bedrock of fundamentalist Christian apologetics. No matter how many contradictions and inconsistencies are thrown up against them from the New Testament, they can always counter with the amazing list of 300 (or 500, or 1000, or more) Old Testament prophecies that were supposedly fulfilled by the life of Jesus. Sometimes this takes the form of some very bad statistical arguments, like the one found on a certain Christian website which calculated the odds of any one individual fulfilling forty of the Old Testament "prophecies" to be one in 10^{157}. Fortunately, all of these alleged prophecies fall into just a few characteristic types, and the general approach for refuting one will generally work for many of the others.

It's important to recognize at the outset that Jesus's name is not mentioned anywhere at all in the Old Testament. Nor does the name Pontius Pilate appear. You also will not find any Old Testament occurrences of the word "crucify" in any form. Consequently, you will never find any Old Testament passage where God says, "I will send my son Jesus to be crucified by Pontius Pilate, and to be raised from the dead on the third day in order to save all people from their sins." There's nothing remotely like this anywhere in the entire Old Testament.

So when the theologians talk of prophecies, they mean that they can take an Old Testament passage which is apparently unrelated to anything in the New Testament, strip it from its original context, and interpret it symbolically to make it appear to predict events recorded in the gospels. This, in essence, is what the Christians are referring to when they speak of Old Testament prophecies. Furthermore, the people who should be best acquainted with the ancient Jewish scriptures, i.e., the Jews themselves, do not recognize the validity of any of these so-called prophecies about Jesus. And throughout the New Testament, Jesus's own relatives and disciples (as distinct from the gospel authors) are confused and puzzled about who he really is, which they should not have been if they had studied their Bible and read the striking "prophecies" which are supposed to be so obvious.

So if there is no direct mention of Jesus or his crucifixion in the Old Testament, and the Jews themselves do not find any such prophecies in their Bible, and if Jesus's own followers did not recognize him as the fulfillment of Old Testament predictions, where did the idea arise that the Hebrew prophets foresaw the coming of Jesus as the Christ? One obvious possibility is that the gospel writers conjured up correspondences between the Old Testament and their own writings about Jesus in order to give Christianity greater legitimacy with the Roman authorities. The Romans were naturally suspicious of new religions, but were generally quite tolerant of those that had an ancient pedigree. Judaism, with its ancient scriptures, qualified of course, but Christianity was the new kid on the block. What better way to obtain legitimacy than by latching onto an existing religious tradition that already had gained acceptance in the Empire? As we shall see, the correspondences are very tenuous, but it was a superstitious age, and the standards for persuasion were not high.

What then are these hundreds of alleged prophecies from the Old Testament? And if they don't mention Jesus, or crucifixion, or Pontius Pilate or rising from the dead, how are they predictive of anything written about Jesus? What we find is that many are not even actual declarative statements. In other words., they don't declare that anything in particular will happen, but are merely phrases or expressions – sentence fragments – from the Old Testament which also appear somewhere in the New Testament. You can do a search[1] on any phrase in the Bible, get some Old Testament results and some New Testament results, and then call the Old Testament results "prophecies" of the New Testament occurrences. That's not much different from a lot of the supposed prophecies cited by the Christians concerning Jesus. Some of the referenced Old Testament passages are misquoted by the New Testament authors, some are capable of voluntary self-fulfillment, and sometimes two or more unrelated passages from the Old Testament (even from different books) are put together and treated as a single "prophecy."

As for the statistical argument, statistics theory only applies to random processes. There is nothing random at all about a process of hunting through the Old Testament to find passages that correspond vaguely with the words in a New Testament passage, and then passing it off as a "prophecy," while ignoring all the other Old Testament passages that tell something different. Remember, when we read the gospels, we are not viewing Jesus's actual life. We are reading what someone *wrote* about Jesus's life, composed decades after the time in which he lived. An author who wanted to claim that Jesus fulfilled Old Testament predictions, and who was familiar with the

---

[1] An excellent site for searching the Bible online is *www.biblegateway.com*.

Hebrew scriptures, could simply add events to his narrative that mirror whatever language or incident he wants to match. From a statistical standpoint, it's not like rolling a pair of dice. It's more like rolling one die, and then deliberately positioning the other one to match what shows up on the first.

Fundamentalists will, of course, reject the idea that the gospel authors could be so dishonest, but if they're trying to use these prophecies to convince the unconvinced, they need to be operating in the world of reason and evidence. In that world, it is always more likely that an author added some phrases to his story to make his argument seem stronger, than that a dead man came alive in accordance with prophecies made hundreds of years earlier.

Obviously we won't be able to consider every single claim of prophecy from the Old Testament, but we'll take a look at several of the more prominent ones to see how they fit the general patterns, and the reasons why we should not be impressed. In the examples that follow, we'll concern ourselves only with prophecies claimed by the gospel writers themselves, and not with any new prophecies "discovered" by Christians in later times.

False prophecy #1: He shall be called a Nazarene.

Matthew 2:23 – "And he came and dwelt in a city called Nazareth: that it might be fulfilled which was spoken by the prophets, He shall be called a Nazarene."

In this passage, the author of Matthew tells us that Joseph took his family, including the baby Jesus, to Nazareth in order to fulfill a prophecy, namely that, "He shall be called a Nazarene." Matthew does not tell us who "he" is when he quotes this passage, but he obviously wants us to think that it refers to the expected messiah.

The problem is that there is no such statement by the prophets or anyone else anywhere in the Old Testament. The city of Nazareth is not even mentioned in the Old Testament, nor is its adjectival form "Nazarene." The assertion in Matthew 2:23 is false, yet Christians claim it as a fulfilled prophecy of Jesus's coming. How do they explain this? Their only recourse is to reinterpret some other passage so that it seems to refer to Nazareth. It turns out that the Hebrew word for "branch" sounds somewhat like "Nazareth."[2] This interpretation allows the Christians to claim that Jeremiah 23:5 may be the missing link: "Behold, the days come, saith the LORD, that I will raise unto David a righteous branch, and a king shall reign and prosper, and shall execute judgment and justice in the earth." It still doesn't say anything about Jesus, but it does contain a word that in Hebrew has some resemblance to "Nazareth." It's kind of like saying that because Adam and Eve ate an apple, this means that the messiah would come from Minne*apol*is. As you can see, it's quite a stretch, like a pun that doesn't quite work.

Furthermore, the Jeremiah passage is obviously referring to an earthly king in the Davidic line, and Jesus was never that. Christians may believe that he will come back to rule the earth someday, but they can't count that as a fulfillment of prophecy, because it hasn't happened yet. The fact of the matter is that Jesus was never a king, and has never ruled over Israel or any other land. So no prophecy about the messiah can be considered to be fulfilled by Jesus. The Christians interpret Isaiah 11:1 in a similar way: "And there shall come forth a rod out of the stem of Jesse [king David's father], and a branch shall grow out of his roots."

---

[2] *The New Oxford Annotated Bible*, p.1173.

Phony Prophecies from the Old Testament

The other common response to this particular false prophecy is to say that "Nazarene" should be understood figuratively as "one who is despised" because of the low level of esteem in which Nazareth was held by other Jewish communities. (See, for example, John 1:46.) But as soon as a fundamentalist Christian resorts to figurative or metaphorical interpretation to resolve a contradiction, they have already abandoned the literal truth of the Bible, and we skeptics have won the debate. And if we are going to interpret anything in the Bible figuratively or metaphorically, why stop at just those passages that cause problems for the literalists? Why not put a metaphorical interpretation on the whole theological edifice from original sin to the crucifixion, resurrection, and the everlasting fires of hell? Besides, as we have already seen, 2 Peter 1:20 warns that no prophecy of scripture is subject to one's own private interpretation.

False prophecy #2: A virgin shall conceive and bear a son.

Isaiah 7:14 – "Therefore the Lord himself shall give you a sign: Behold, a virgin [or "young woman"] shall conceive, and bear a son, and shall call his name Immanuel."

Matthew 1:22-23 – "Now all this was done, that it might be fulfilled which was spoken of the Lord by the prophet, saying, Behold, a virgin shall be with child, and shall bring forth a son, and they shall call his name Emmanuel, which being interpreted is, God with us."

This is another example of the Christians choosing only those parts of a passage that support their claim and ignoring the rest. The debate rages back and forth as to whether "young woman" or "virgin" is the correct translation in Isaiah, and plausible arguments can be raised on both sides. But the last part of the quotation makes this

143

debate pointless, because Jesus was obviously not called Immanuel. So this passage cannot refer to Jesus. The fundamentalists can have their "virgin" in this passage and it doesn't help their position one bit. For not only is the name wrong, but this is also a "prophecy" that is capable of self-fulfillment. By simply adding some lines about a virgin birth in the gospels, you can create a "fulfilled prophecy." All this shows is that the writers of Matthew and Luke were able to write a story using phrases similar to those found in the Isaiah passage. This refutation can be applied to many of the alleged prophecies, because the "evidence" for their fulfillment is nothing more than an assertion on the part of the gospel writers that the "predicted" event happened. As you can well imagine, these authors are not exactly unbiased witnesses. Unless there is independent verification of the fulfillment, it is necessarily suspect. In any case, Jesus was not called Immanuel, so this prophetic claim is false. And it doesn't help to argue that the name Immanuel means "God with us" and since Jesus was God and was with us, Jesus was in some sense "Immanuel." For Isaiah 7:14 does not say that the *meaning* of the name Immanuel will apply to the child, but that his *name* will be Immanuel.

The Christian claim becomes even more far-fetched when we examine the context of Isaiah 7:14. The verse occurs in the context of a story where the Davidic king Ahaz fears an imminent attack by two enemies. The birth of the child in verse 7:14 is part of a promise from Yahweh that the lands of the two enemies feared by Ahaz will be deserted "before the child shall know to refuse the evil and choose the good." (Isaiah 7:16) So obviously the child was to be born during the time of this conflict, which was centuries before the birth of Jesus. And surely Jesus, if he truly was God, would have already known how to "refuse the evil and choose the good." So the Isaiah child, who has to learn these things, cannot possibly be identified with Jesus. Isaiah 7:14 is therefore a phony prophecy which has absolutely nothing to do with Jesus of Nazareth.

False prophecy #3: Out of Egypt have I called my son.

Hosea 11:1 – "When Israel was a child, then I loved him, and called my son out of Egypt."

Matthew 2:14-15 – Joseph rose and "took the young child and his mother by night, and departed into Egypt, and was there until the death of Herod, that it might be fulfilled which was spoken of the Lord by the prophet, saying, Out of Egypt have I called my son."

The passage from Hosea continues: "they sacrificed unto Baalim [pagan gods], and burned incense to graven images." (Hosea 11:2) So if Hosea 11:1 refers to Jesus, this subsequent verse surely does as well. Do the Christians then want us to believe that Jesus, the "son" who was called out of Egypt, also sacrificed to pagan gods and worshipped graven images? In fact, these verses from Hosea obviously do not point to Jesus at all, but to the nation of Israel whom Moses led out of Egypt. The continuation in Hosea 11:2 calls attention to the sin and wickedness of the Hebrews as they strayed from Yahweh's commandments. Are we then to understand that this sin and wickedness apply to Jesus, too? How about Hosea 11:6, which predicts that "the sword shall abide on his cities, and shall consume his branches, and devour them." Does this mean that the "branch" we encountered earlier in false prophecy #1, and which supposedly represents the messiah, will be destroyed so there will be no messiah after all? If these continuation verses, which are all part of the same narrative, have no reference to Jesus of Nazareth, then 11:1 obviously has nothing to do with him either, and therefore the claim of prophecy in Matthew 2:14-15 is completely false.

This is a perfect example of how the Christians pick passages out of context to support their claim of prophecy, while ignoring those passages that do not fit their interpretation. If Hosea 11:1 really refers to Jesus, then the whole story must apply to him, not just the pieces that are convenient for the Christians. But the passages that describe sacrificing to false gods and turning away from the LORD clash with the portrayal of Jesus in the gospels.

And as we have already seen, the Matthew story of the flight into Egypt is directly contradicted by Luke's account of Jesus's birth, which has Jesus and his family going directly to Jerusalem with no detour into Egypt. So if Hosea 11:1 is taken as a *bona fide* prophecy that Jesus must sojourn in Egypt, then Luke's account, which rules out any trip to Egypt, must be seen as a failure of that prophecy. There is no way out of this dilemma, because of the conflicting birth stories told by Matthew and Luke.

False prophecy #4: He took our infirmities and bore our diseases.

Isaiah 53:4 – "Surely he has borne our griefs, and carried our sorrows. Yet we did esteem him stricken, smitten of God, and afflicted." (The RSV gives alternative translations for griefs and sorrows as "sicknesses" and "pains.")[3]

Matthew 8:16-17 – "When the evening had come, they brought unto him many that were possessed with devils. And he cast out the spirits with his word, and healed all that were sick; that it might be fulfilled which was spoken by Isaiah the prophet, saying, He himself took our infirmities, and bore our sicknesses."

---

[3] *The New Oxford Annotated Bible,* p.889.

But in Matthew's narrative, Jesus did not bear the diseases himself. He simply made them go away. So the correspondence with Isaiah is inexact. If Isaiah predicted anything at all here, he predicted that the people's diseases would be borne by this individual, not cured. There is a bigger problem here, however. The reference in Isaiah is not to Jesus, but to the nation of Israel as God's servant. This becomes obvious if you read the entire context from chapter 40 through 56. Isaiah is not describing an itinerant medical practitioner, but the suffering servant of Yahweh. Christians believe the servant referred to in the 53rd chapter of Isaiah is Jesus, and they claim to find numerous instances in that chapter of what they believe to be prophetic references to him. They are all subject to the same refutations, so let's consider them together.

False prophecy #5: The suffering Servant of Isaiah 53.

Isaiah 53:3 – "He is despised and rejected of men; a man of sorrows, and acquainted with grief: and we hid as it were our faces from him; he was despised, and we esteemed him not."

Isaiah 53:5 – "But he was wounded for our transgressions. He was bruised for our iniquities. The chastisement of our peace was upon him; and with his stripes we are healed."

Isaiah 53:7 – "He was oppressed, and he was afflicted, yet he opened not his mouth: he is brought as a lamb to the slaughter, and as a sheep before her shearers is dumb [i.e., mute, unable to speak], so he openeth not his mouth."

Isaiah 53:10-12 – "Yet it pleased the LORD to bruise him; he has put him to grief. When you shall make his soul an offering for sin, he shall see his seed [i.e., his offspring], he shall prolong his days, and the pleasure of the LORD shall prosper in his hand. He shall see of the travail of his soul, and shall be satisfied. By his knowledge shall my righteous servant justify many, for he shall bear their iniquities. Therefore will I divide him a portion with the great, and he shall divide the spoil with the strong; because he has poured out his soul unto death: and he was numbered with the transgressors; and he bore the sin of many, and made intercession for the transgressors."

If all you know from the Bible is the story of Jesus, then you will certainly see a resemblance with these passages taken out of context from Isaiah. But was the author of Isaiah really talking about Jesus, and was he specifically foretelling a divine Jesus who was sent by Yahweh to save the world from its sins? It's easy to answer these questions, because the answers are contained in the book of Isaiah itself. You just have to go back to chapter 40 and read up to chapter 53 to get the whole context, which explains the identity of the servant.

It turns out that chapters 40 through 56 of Isaiah are about the liberation of the Jews from the Babylonian captivity and their return to Palestine, thanks to the conquest of Babylon by the Persian king Cyrus. This all occurred during the 6th century BC. Throughout these chapters, there is reference to the "servant" of God, which is identified with Israel. Yahweh assures Israel that its time of suffering is now over and that it will soon bask in the honor and admiration of all the nations that previously had oppressed it. It is a poetic rendering, and is broken into four "Servant songs" spoken variously by Yahweh, the personified nation of Israel, or the author/prophet himself. Christians want to identify the servant with Jesus, and to connect with him the passages relating to Israel's salvation and the bearing of its sins. Of course, the name of Jesus is not mentioned in Isaiah at all, so the entire Christian argument is based on interpretation (again). When we read the book of Isaiah as a whole, and not as isolated verses picked out of context, we can easily see that the Servant is Israel, not Jesus, and Yahweh himself is the Holy One of Israel, as well as its only redeemer and savior.

Israel, not Jesus, is the servant referred to in Isaiah chapters 40-56:

- "But *you, Israel, are my servant*, Jacob whom I have chosen, the seed of Abraham my friend. You whom I have taken from the ends of the earth, and called you from the chief men thereof, and said unto you, *You are my servant*; I have chosen you, and not cast you away." (Isaiah 41:8-9)
- "Now hear, O Jacob my servant; and Israel, whom I have chosen!" (Isaiah 44:1)
- "Remember these, O Jacob and Israel; for you are my servant. I have formed you; you are my servant: O Israel, you shall not be forgotten by me." (Isaiah 44:21)
- "You are my servant, O Israel, in whom I will be glorified." (Isaiah 49:3)

So reading the full story tells us that Jesus is not the servant – Israel is the servant. Also, there is the small matter that if Jesus is the servant of God, then he cannot possibly be co-equal with God, as Trinitarian theology would have it. Jesus would instead be inferior to God, as this is the essential nature of a servant's relationship to his master. Note as well that in the passages quoted at the beginning of this section, all the suffering of the servant is in the past tense – i.e., past at the time of the Isaiah writing. Prophecies are about the future, so the fact that the servant *was* despised and rejected by men, or *was* afflicted and *opened* not his mouth, shows that these things have already occurred by the time Isaiah was writing them. This makes perfect sense if he's writing about Israel's history of oppression and suffering, but is totally inconsistent with the idea of predicting the future.

A further difficulty in trying to equate Jesus with Isaiah's servant, is that the servant "shall see his seed" [i.e., his offspring, descendants] (Isaiah 53:10), but Jesus never had any offspring, at least not any that we're told about. Christians try to get around this by considering the church as Jesus's "offspring" but this is just a desperation argument that requires us to take a metaphorical interpretation of Isaiah's language. Once they do that, the literalists have lost the point, because they are again substituting their own interpretations for the literal wording of the Bible.

We are told elsewhere in Isaiah that the servant "shall not cry, nor lift up, nor cause his voice to be heard in the street." (Isaiah 42:2) Amazingly, this passage is actually cited as a prophecy by the Christians as well, even though the gospel accounts of Jesus directly contradict it. Mark and Matthew both tell us that Jesus "cried with a loud voice" while on the cross, saying "My God, my God, why hast thou forsaken me?" (Mark 15:34; Matthew 27:46. See also Luke 23:46.)

Yahweh [God], not Jesus, is the holy one of Israel, and its redeemer and savior:

- "For I am the LORD your God, the Holy One of Israel, your saviour." (Isaiah 43:3)
- "Thus says the LORD, your redeemer, the Holy One of Israel." (Isaiah 43:14)
- "I am the LORD, your Holy One, the creator of Israel, your king." (Isaiah 43:15)

- "I am he who blots out your transgressions for my own sake, and will not remember your sins." (Isaiah 43:25)
- "Thus says the LORD the king of Israel, and his redeemer the LORD of hosts; I am the first, and I am the last; and beside me there is no God." (Isaiah 44:6)
- "I have blotted out, as a thick cloud, your transgressions, and, as a cloud, your sins. Return unto me; for I have redeemed you." (Isaiah 44:22) [And if God could sweep away sins so easily, why was there any need for Jesus to come and save the world from its sins?]
- "Israel shall be saved in the LORD with an everlasting salvation." (Isaiah 45:17)
- "There is no God else beside me; a just God and a Saviour; there is none beside me." (Isaiah 45:21)
- "As for our redeemer, the LORD of hosts is his name, the Holy One of Israel." (Isaiah 47:4)
- "Thus says the LORD, the redeemer of Israel and his Holy One." (Isaiah 49:7)
- "I the LORD am your Saviour and your Redeemer, the mighty One of Jacob." (Isaiah 49:26)

Remember that the LORD, in capital letters, is how English translations translate YHWH, the Hebrew name for God, which with vowels is rendered into English as Yahweh. It is not to be confused with "the Lord" as used in the New Testament to refer to Jesus.

Thus, we have seen that Israel, not Jesus, is the suffering servant of Yahweh. Yahweh, not Jesus, is the redeemer and savior of Israel. Isaiah chapter 53 does not refer to Jesus in any way at all, and certainly not as either God's servant, nor as the savior of mankind. Any New Testament references to the suffering servant of Isaiah being a prophecy of Jesus as the savior of Israel, or of mankind, are demonstrably false, based on the plain language and full context of Isaiah.

The messiah identified by name!

But in the book of Isaiah there is one specific reference to the anointed one, the messiah, who is to deliver Israel from its oppressors. He is even mentioned by name. *But the name is not Jesus.* It is Cyrus, king of Persia. "Thus says the LORD to his anointed, to Cyrus." (Isaiah 45:1) Remember that "anointed" is the meaning of the Hebrew word "messiah." Furthermore, God says of Cyrus, "He is my shepherd and will accomplish all that I please; he will say of Jerusalem, 'Let it be rebuilt,' and of the temple, 'Let its foundations be laid.'" (Isaiah 44:28) (NIV) If Cyrus was to fulfill *all* God's purpose, that doesn't leave much of a role for Jesus to play. So Cyrus, the Persian, the non-Jew, was to be God's chosen instrument for releasing the Israelites from their Babylonian captivity. It is doubtful whether Cyrus himself knew of this great honor, but he did in fact conquer Babylon and open the way for the restoration of the Jews to their Palestinian homeland. The fall of Babylon took place in the year 539 BC, carried out by Cyrus, the anointed one of God, without any help from Jesus.

False prophecy #6: Riding on a donkey.

Zechariah 9:9 – "Behold, your king is coming to you; he is just and endowed with salvation, humble, and mounted on a donkey." (NASB)

John 12:14 – "Jesus, finding a young donkey, sat on it; as it is written." (NASB)

Well, how else would he have arrived – in a Corvette? Donkeys were a common mode of transport in ancient times[4], so Jesus is probably not the only one who entered

---

[4] Oded Borowski, *Every Living Thing: Daily Use of Animals in Ancient Israel* (Alta Mira Press, 1998), pp.95-97.

Jerusalem on a donkey. There is nothing remarkable at all in this event.

Also, this passage falls into the category of self-fulfillable prophecies. If you know that the messiah is supposed to come riding on a donkey, you would probably hop on a donkey and go to town, just so you could claim to be the messiah. So even if it were true, and even if it were a prophecy, its fulfillment would be trivial, and not at all impressive. Perhaps we should try to identify all the other individuals who rode into Jerusalem on a donkey, because each of them would have just as much claim to be the messiah.

This is another passage where seeing the full context takes away much of the force from the alleged prophecy by supplying additional details that do not mesh with the Christians' prophetic interpretation. The continuation in Zechariah 9:10 is "I will cut off the chariot from Ephraim and the horse from Jerusalem; and the bow of war shall be cut off, and he shall speak peace to the nations; his dominion will be from sea to sea, and from the river to the ends of the earth." (NASB) Thus, if this were a fulfilled prophecy about Jesus, he would have ended war and brought peace to all nations in ruling over them, including in Jerusalem. But Jesus did not bring peace. He did not even claim that that was his purpose: "Think not that I have come to send peace on earth. I came not to send peace, but a sword." (Matthew 10:34) (Also see Luke 12:51) There has indeed been much fighting in the name of Jesus, and just a few decades after he lived, in 70 AD, Jerusalem itself was destroyed by the Romans. So there is no way that Jesus could possibly be the bringer of peace referred to in Zechariah 9:9-10.

False prophecy #7: The price of Judas's betrayal.

Zechariah 11:12-13 – "So they weighed for my price thirty pieces of silver. And the LORD said unto me, Cast it unto the potter: a goodly price that I was prised at of them. And I took the thirty pieces of silver, and cast them to the potter in the house of the LORD."

Matthew 27:5-10 – "And he cast down the pieces of silver in the temple, and departed, and went and hanged himself. And the chief priests took the silver pieces, and said, It is not lawful for to put them into the treasury, because it is the price of blood. And they took counsel, and bought with them the potter's field, to bury strangers in. Wherefore that field was called, The field of blood, unto this day. Then was fulfilled that which was spoken by Jeremy the prophet, saying, 'And they took the thirty pieces of silver, the price of him that was valued, whom they of the children of Israel did value, and gave them for the potter's field, as the Lord appointed me.'"

Matthew wrongly attributes this alleged prophecy to Jeremiah. There is nothing in Jeremiah that mentions thirty pieces of silver. There is one reference in Jeremiah to the purchase of a field, but in that case the price was seventeen shekels of silver, not thirty: "And I bought the field of Hanameel my uncle's son, that was in Anathoth, and weighed him the money, even seventeen shekels of silver." (Jeremiah 32:9) The closest we can get to an Old Testament source for Matthew's claim is the passage quoted above from Zechariah 11:12-13, but in Zechariah, the thirty shekels are the wages of a shepherd, who is doing the work of Yahweh. There's nothing in the passage from Zechariah to connect the thirty shekels with any story of betrayal. And there's no reason to connect these thirty pieces of silver to Judas, other than the coincidence of the amount. In Exodus

21:32, thirty shekels of silver is the price to be paid as restitution if an ox gores another man's slave – in addition to which the ox shall be stoned. I haven't run across any attempts to turn the Exodus passage into a prophecy of Judas's betrayal, but that doesn't mean no one's tried.

In any event, the appearance of a particular sum of money, in this case thirty shekels of silver, in both the Old Testament and the New Testament is hardly evidence of a prophecy. There are many other amounts of money mentioned in the Old Testament. Should we consider those to be failed prophecies because they don't match the thirty pieces of silver in the Judas story? In 2 Samuel 24:24 we find that "David bought the threshing floor and the oxen for fifty shekels of silver." Is this a prophecy of the price paid for Judas's betrayal? There's just as much reason to consider this a prophecy of Judas's price as the passage from Zechariah. In Genesis 37:28, Joseph was sold to the Ishmaelites for twenty shekels of silver. Why isn't this considered a prophecy of the Judas betrayal? If these other passages are prophecies of Judas, then they are wrong, because the amounts don't match. But if these are not prophecies, then neither is the passage from Zechariah, because Zechariah's words have no closer connection to Judas than the others do.

What you see here is a common fallacy perpetrated by Christians in their attempts to persuade others that the Old Testament really does predict the coming of Jesus. They find passages in the Old Testament that correspond somewhat to New Testament events, and call those fulfilled prophecies. But other Old Testament passages, no more remote than the ones they've chosen, which contradict New Testament events, are ignored rather than being treated as failed prophecies. The method is deceptive and logically fallacious.

False prophecy #8: *Not a bone of him shall be broken.*

Exodus 12:46 – *"And you shall not break a bone of it." (RSV) (Referring to the Passover meal. See also Numbers 9:12)*

Psalm 34:20 – *"He keeps all his bones; not one of them is broken."*

John 19:33,36 – *"But when they came to Jesus, and saw that he was dead already, they broke not his legs. . . . For these things were done, that the scripture should be fulfilled: 'A bone of him shall not be broken.'"*

Here again, there are competing Old Testament passages, and the Christians have picked the ones that fit their story. Here are the ones they didn't tells us about:

Lamentations 3:4 – *"My flesh and my skin he has made old; he has **broken my bones**."*

Psalm 51:8 – *"Make me to hear joy and gladness; that the **bones which you have broken** may rejoice."*

If these verses are the prophecy, instead of those previously quoted, then John 19:36 contradicts them, and the prophecy is false. So take your choice. The Old Testament writings contain a wide variety of circumstances, phrases and meanings, and you can usually find one to fit almost any New Testament circumstance you want.

False prophecy #9: *On the third day he will raise us up.*

Hosea 6:2 – *"After two days will he revive us: in the third day he will raise us up and we shall live in his sight."*

Phony Prophecies from the Old Testament

Luke 18:31-33 – "All things that are written by the prophets concerning the Son of man shall be accomplished. For he shall be delivered unto the Gentiles, and shall be mocked, and spitefully entreated, and spitted on. And they shall scourge him, and put him to death, and the third day he shall rise again."

The link here is somewhat tenuous, but perhaps Luke has this passage from Hosea in mind, as there do not appear to be any other passages from the prophets or anywhere else in the Old Testament that come close, and Luke himself does not say which prophets he's referring to. However, the link fails, because Hosea cannot be referring to Jesus, nor to any single individual, for the pronoun "he" explicitly refers to Yahweh in verse 6:1, and the pronouns "we" and "us" are all plural. He will revive *us*. And he will raise *us* up, that *we* may live in his sight. So it cannot mean Jesus individually who is being raised up on the third day. The reference in Hosea is once again to the people of Israel, who have strayed from the LORD's commandments. Yahweh himself is speaking in this quotation, speaking as the Israelites might speak if they should ever return to the path commanded by Yahweh. One can hardly imagine that the Christians really believe that this image of the wayward, sinful people actually refers to Jesus. This is another instance of a passage taken out of context, to mean something other than what it originally intended.

False prophecy #10: As the prophets and Moses have said.

Acts 26:22-23 – "I continue unto this day, witnessing both to small and great, saying none other things than those which the prophets and Moses did say should come: That Christ should suffer, and that he should be the first that

157

should rise from the dead, and should show light unto the people, and to the Gentiles."

There is no such passage in Moses or the prophets. As we have seen, there is no mention of "Jesus" anywhere in the Old Testament, so there cannot be any passage that predicts his suffering or resurrection. "Christ" is equivalent to the Hebrew "messiah," meaning the anointed one, and was used frequently in the Old Testament to refer to the Hebrew kings. But there are no passages that refer to the "Christ" as suffering and rising from the dead. Indeed there are passages containing just the opposite message, that Yahweh will protect his anointed: "Touch not my anointed ones, and do my prophets no harm." (1 Chronicles 16:22; Psalm 105:15)

And contrary to this passage from Acts, Jesus Christ was not the first to rise from the dead. According to the gospels, Lazarus (John 11:43-44), the ruler's little girl (Matthew 9:18, 23-25), and the widow's son (Luke 7:12-15) already were raised from the dead before Jesus. There is also an Old Testament story about Elisha raising a child from the dead. (2 Kings 4:32-35)

Prophecies that the Theologians Never Told Us About

Employing the same methods used by the Christians, it's possible to find all sorts of "prophecies" hidden in the Old Testament writings. Humorous examples include Old Testament passages that foretell the rise of Napoleon, and the golf successes of Tiger Woods. One of the wittiest examples of this genre is Moshe Shulman's discovery that the Old Testament amazingly foretold the pursuit, capture, slaughter, cooking, and eating of his rooster which was served up for dinner on the day before Yom Kippur.[5] An amusing pastime is to see what other individuals' lives, famous or not, were actually "prophesied" in the Old Testament.

But apart from these humorous uses of Christian prophetic methods, it is also possible using these same methods to find numerous prophecies in the Old Testament warning us against the false prophet Jesus. The fact that we can do this makes it obvious that the many alleged prophecies cited by the Christian apologists actually prove nothing at all. They do not refer to Jesus, either explicitly or implicitly. They almost never refer to any future event, which any true prediction would have to do. Many are not even factual statements, but commands or exhortations. And many are capable of self-fulfillment by anyone who wants to look like the messiah. You can really "prophesy" anything at all using the same sources and the same methods used by the Christians to find "hundreds" of prophecies relating to Jesus in the Old Testament. As a final example, here's what the Old Testament warns us to watch for regarding the false prophet Jesus.

Old Testament warnings against following Jesus:

"*I am the* LORD *[Yahweh], and besides me there is no saviour."* (Isaiah 43:11)

"*I am the* LORD *your God from the land of Egypt, and you shall know no god but me: for there is no saviour beside me."* (Hosea 13:4)

---

[5] Moshe Shulman, "A Chassidic Rabbi Makes a Startling Discovery." *http://www.qumran.org/js/texts/mrooster.php.*

Thus, by claiming to be mankind's savior, Jesus committed blasphemy against the LORD, who is the only true savior.

"They have no knowledge that set up the wood of their graven image [i.e., the cross], and pray unto a god that cannot save." (Isaiah 45:20)

"As a thief is shamed when caught, so the house of Israel shall be shamed: they, their kings, their princes, their priests, and their prophets, who say to a tree 'You are my father." (Jeremiah 2:26-27)

The "wood" and the "tree" are obvious references to the cross. This is a clear warning against idolizing an inanimate object (the cross) and the false god Jesus associated with it. In Jesus, blasphemy and idolatry are united.

"And if a man has committed a sin worthy of death, and he be to be put to death, and you hang him on a tree. his body shall not remain all night upon the tree, but you shall in any wise bury him that day; for he that is hanged is accursed of God." (Deuteronomy 21:22-23)

But Jesus himself was hanged on a tree: Acts 10:39 tells of Jesus "whom they slew and hanged on a tree." Therefore, Jesus was accursed by God. See also Acts 5:30 and 13:29 for additional references to hanging Jesus on a tree.

"Thus says the LORD: Write this man childless, a man that shall not prosper in his days: for no man of his seed shall prosper, sitting upon the throne of David, and ruling any more in Judah.." (Jeremiah 22:30)

Jesus's actions in the New Testament completely fulfill this prophecy. He was indeed childless, and he certainly did not succeed in his days, for he was crucified and even his own disciples did not understand his message. Furthermore, he had no offspring who sat on the throne of David, and Jesus himself, despite claims of messiahship, never ruled as king of Israel.

"The men of Memphis and Tahpanhes have broken the crown of your head. Have you not brought this upon yourself by forsaking the Lord your God when he led you in the way? (Jeremiah 2:16-17) (RSV)

Obviously this is a prophecy of Matthew 27:29-30 where after setting the crown of thorns, the Roman soldiers beat Jesus about the head, which likely would have broken the crown. Although Jesus complained that God had forsaken him (Mark 15:34), it was actually Jesus who had forsaken the ways of God.

"But the remainder of the flesh of the sacrifice on the third day shall be burnt with fire." (Leviticus 7:17)

This verse tells us what really happened to Jesus's body. He did not rise from the dead on the third day, but actually was sent to burn in hell for his blasphemy.

"All the kings of the nations, even all of them, lie in glory, every one in his own house. But you are cast out of your grave like an abominable branch, and as the raiment of those that are slain, thrust through with a sword, that go down to the stones of the pit; as a carcass trodden under feet." (Isaiah 14:18-19)

This passage fits perfectly with events described in the gospels. After the crucifixion, his body was missing from his tomb – i.e., cast out of his grave. (Luke 24:3; John 20:2) While on the cross, Jesus was pierced by the Roman soldiers. (John 19:34) And if "branch" in Jeremiah 23:5 and Isaiah 11:1 (see under false prophecy #1) are indications of Jesus's Nazarene origins, as the Christians would have us believe, then Isaiah 14:19, which refers to an "abominable

The Atheist's Introduction to the New Testament

branch," is a clear rejection of Jesus as the Davidic messiah. These verses express Yahweh's anger at Jesus's false preaching, as well as his claim to messiahship, and foretell his death and empty tomb, which were signs of disgrace in the eyes of God.

"Who are you, that you should be afraid of a man that shall die, and of the son of man which shall be made as grass, and forget the LORD your maker, who has stretched forth the heavens, and laid the foundations of the earth?" (Isaiah 51:12-13)

Here, God warns us against following the "son of man," which was the phrase most often used by Jesus when referring to himself.

"God is not a man, that He should lie, neither the son of man, that He should repent." (Numbers 23:19)

Again, "Son of man" was the phrase used by Jesus to refer to himself. In this passage from Numbers, we are warned that the son of man is not God, and that God does not take human form.

"The gods that have not made the heavens and the earth, even they shall perish from the earth, and from under these heavens." (Jeremiah 10:11)

There is only one God, and he created the heavens and the earth. (Isaiah 45:18) But Jesus said "I came down from heaven." (John 6:38) And his followers equated him with the Creator himself. (Colossians 1:15-16) In this prophecy, Jeremiah rightly foretold that such false gods would "perish from the earth," as Jesus did when he was executed by the Romans. This would also explain why the second coming never occurred.

"He feeds on ashes; a deluded mind has led him astray."
(Isaiah 44:20) (RSV)

This is confirmed in Mark 3:21, where even in Jesus's hometown people were saying, "He is beside himself."

Try running these passages past a Christian and see what kind of reaction you get. Most likely they will pull out their Bible, look up the references, and tell you that these verses were taken out of context, or that they don't refer to Jesus, or that we are wrongly interpreting them. But how is that any different from the passages that the Christians claim are prophetic of Jesus's coming? It's not different at all. The truth is that there are no prophecies of Jesus in the Old Testament. There is only a vast collection of stories, and sentences, and parts of sentences that can be plucked out, rearranged, and matched up with some of the New Testament verses to create the illusion of prophecy. Looking backwards, with 20/20 hindsight, we are all prophets.

Chapter 11: Fighting Dirty - How to Use Ad Hominem Arguments Against Christian Hypocrites

The contradictions that we've looked at so far are enough to convince any logical, open-minded person that the Christian religion is a hodgepodge of self-contradictory messages. Using this evidence, you should be able easily to win any debate against Christian fundamentalists who believe in the literal truth of the Bible. But as we all know, not every opponent is rational. What do you do against an opponent who's impervious to logic? Unfortunately, these opponents can achieve great rhetorical effect, especially in front of an unschooled audience, by using logically unsound arguments. One such tactic is the argument *ad hominem*. An ad hominem argument is one that attacks the messenger instead of the message. It asserts that a proposition must be false because the person delivering it is a rogue, scoundrel, or hypocrite, or morally deficient in some way. But the proposition may still be true, in spite of the personal failings of its proponent. Thus, the ad hominem argument is a logical fallacy.

But the ad hominem argument comes up frequently in religious debate. It is not always precisely stated, but can take various forms of expression, such as:

- "Just look at Hitler and Stalin and you'll see what happens to a country run by atheists."
- "You use the Bible to argue against Christianity, yet you yourself don't even believe in the Bible!"
- "How can you criticize the Church, when you don't even go to church?"

In each of these cases, the attack is turned against the specific individual who expresses a position, not against the validity of the position itself. Note that if an atheist critic of Christianity suddenly started going to Church, that would have no impact at all on whether the Church's doctrines were true or beneficial.

The argument can work the other way, too: "You say our country needs to be founded on Christian principles, but you drink, smoke, and cuss. Why should I believe a hypocrite like you?"

This argument is just as fallacious as the previous one, because it avoids coming to terms with the stated proposition, which holds that the country should be founded on Christian principles, and instead attacks the behavior of the individuals who support those principles.

Ad hominem is a fallacious argument that has no place in rational dialogue. But as you may have noticed, religious discussion does not always take place within a rational framework. Many Christians will use distortions and fallacious arguments to great rhetorical effect when debating against nonbelievers. So if you choose to respond on those terms, this chapter gives you some ammunition that comes straight from the New Testament itself. These verses will support two approaches: 1) discrediting the Christian apologists on the grounds that they themselves do not follow Christian principles – i.e., that they are hypocrites; and 2) associating your Christian opponents with political views that are widely considered to be immoral or unjust, such as slavery and the inferiority of women.

Christian Hypocrisy: Biblical principles violated by most Christians

Riches and the Kingdom of Heaven

Rich people do not get much positive press in the New Testament. In fact, being well-to-do is a positive obstacle to getting into the kingdom of God. Chances are that you don't know any Christians at all who follow the New Testament teachings about material wealth. If you do, they probably live in a monastery or convent. But if you take the Bible seriously, any Christian whose living standard is above that of Mother Theresa has some explaining to do. So ask them to explain why they don't follow these precepts:

- "If you would be perfect, go and sell what you have and give to the poor, and you will have treasure in heaven." (Matthew 19:21)

Here the Christians may respond, "Ah, but that's if you want to be *perfect*. God knows that humans are not perfect, so he doesn't really expect us to live up to this standard." Well, yes he does: "Be ye therefore perfect, even as your Father which is in heaven is perfect." (Matthew 5:48)

And in spite of the televangelists who preach that material wealth is a sign of God's favor, you can't have it both ways: "You cannot serve God and mammon."[1] (Matthew 6:24; Luke 16:13)

The same message against the rich is repeated again and again throughout the New Testament:

- "Then said Jesus unto his disciples, Verily I say unto you, That a rich man shall hardly enter into the kingdom

---

[1] "Mammon is a Semitic word for money or riches." *The New Oxford Annotated Bible*, p.1178.

of heaven. And again I say unto you, It is easier for a camel to go through the eye of a needle,[2] than for a rich man to enter into the kingdom of God." (Matthew 19:23-24; also Luke 18:24-25.)
- "Lay not up for yourselves treasures upon earth, where moth and rust corrupt, and where thieves break through and steal: But lay up for yourselves treasures in heaven, where neither moth nor rust corrupts, and where thieves do not break through nor steal: For where your treasure is, there will your heart be also." (Matthew 6:19-21)
- "But they that will be rich fall into temptation and a snare, and into many foolish and hurtful lusts, which drown men in destruction and perdition. For the love of money is the root of all evil." (1 Timothy 6:9-10)
- "You say, 'I am rich, and increased with goods, and have need of nothing,' and know not that you are wretched, and miserable, and poor, and blind, and naked." (Revelation 3:17)

Citing so many passages to prove one point may seem like overkill, but Christians often charge that skeptics argue against the Bible by taking passages out of context. By showing them numerous verses that all contain the same message, from multiple biblical authors, you can effectively refute that counterargument.

And speaking of storing up riches, how did the early apostles live? Well, according to the author of Acts, they were communists: "And all that believed were together, and had all things common; and sold their possessions and

---

[2] "Some interpreters have tried to weaken the rigor of Jesus' words by claiming that the needle's eye was the name of a small gate in the wall that surrounded the city of Jerusalem or that camel is a mistake in the Greek text for a word that means 'rope' or 'cable.' Neither suggestion carries conviction." (*The Interpreter's Bible,* vol. 8, p.314-315.)

goods, and parted them to all men, as every man had need." (Acts 2:44-45) How many Christians do you know who follow this example? Ask them why they don't.

War, Peace, Revenge, and Judgment

There's a strong message of pacifism in the New Testament. For those Christians who think that every foreign policy problem has a military solution, or who support capital punishment, or who hate homosexuals, ask how they square their political position with these messages of love, tolerance, and non-violence found in their own Bible:

- "The fruit of righteousness is sown in peace of them that make peace." (James 3:18)
- "Avenge not yourselves . . . for it is written, 'Vengeance is mine; I will repay,' saith the Lord." (Romans 12:19)
- "But I say unto you which hear, Love your enemies, do good to them which hate you, bless them that curse you, and pray for them which despitefully use you. And unto him that strikes you on the one cheek offer also the other." (Luke 6:27-29)
- "Love your enemies, bless them that curse you, do good to them that hate you, and pray for them which despitefully use you, and persecute you." (Matthew 5:44)
- "Resist not evil: but whoever shall strike you on your right cheek, turn to him the other also." (Matthew 5:39)
- "For if you love those who love you, what reward have you? Do not even the tax collectors do the same? And if you salute only your brethren, what more are you doing than others? Do not even the Gentiles do the same?" (Matthew 5:46-47) (RSV)

- "Put up again your sword into its place: for all they that take the sword shall perish with the sword." (Matthew 26:52)
- "He that kills with the sword must be killed with the sword." (Revelation 13:10)

Judging your neighbor

For the Christian busybodies who presume to judge how others should live their private lives:

- "Who are you that you judge your neighbor?" (James 4:12) (RSV)
- "Judge not, that you be not judged. For with what judgment you judge, you shall be judged: and with what measure you mete, it shall be measured to you again. And why do you behold the speck that is in your brother's eye, but consider not the beam that is in your own eye?" (Matthew 7:1-3)
- "Judge not, and you shall not be judged. Condemn not, and you shall not be condemned. Forgive, and you shall be forgiven: Give, and it shall be given unto you." (Luke 6:37-38)
- "Therefore you are inexcusable, O man, whoever you are that judges. For wherein you judge another, you condemn yourself; for you who judge do the same things." (Romans 2:1)

How to pray:

Jesus gave very clear instructions on how to pray. Surprisingly, he did not advise his followers to pray for riches, Super Bowl victories, weight loss, romantic happiness, protection from hurricanes and tornadoes, or winning lottery tickets. The next time you hear a Christian pray for any of these things, or anything else specific, ask them why they are not following this teaching of Jesus:

- "But when you pray, use not vain repetitions, as the heathen do. For they think that they shall be heard for their much speaking. Be not therefore like them. For your Father knows what things you have need of, before you ask him. After this manner therefore pray:
Our Father which art in heaven, hallowed be thy name. Thy kingdom come, Thy will be done in earth, as it is in heaven. Give us this day our daily bread. And forgive us our debts, as we forgive our debtors. And lead us not into temptation, but deliver us from evil: For thine is the kingdom, and the power, and the glory, for ever. Amen." (Matthew 6:7-13)

Family values?

Fundamentalist Christians are well-known for their devotion to "family values." Usually this means a particular type of family structure that just happens to coincide with their own. An important political goal of the Christian right is to have these "family values" enacted into public policy so that we all can benefit from them. But both Jesus and Paul expressed anti-marriage, anti-family positions, that have nothing in common with the so-called family values espoused by the Christian right. So why don't the fundamentalists follow these values instead?

- "Think not that I have come to send peace on earth. I came not to send peace, but a sword. For I have come to set a man at variance against his father, and the daughter against her mother, and the daughter in law against her mother in law. And a man's foes shall be they of his own household." (Matthew 10:34-36)
- "If any man comes to me, and hates not his father, and mother, and wife, and children, and brothers, and sisters, yea, and his own life also, he cannot be my disciple." (Luke 14:26)

- "And call no man your father upon the earth: for one is your Father, which is in heaven." (Matthew 23:9)
- "Do you suppose that I have come to give peace on earth? I tell you, No; but rather division. For from henceforth there shall be five in one house divided, three against two, and two against three. The father shall be divided against the son, and the son against the father; the mother against the daughter, and the daughter against the mother; the mother in law against her daughter in law, and the daughter in law against her mother in law." (Luke 12:51-53)
- Those who marry "shall have trouble in the flesh." (1 Corinthians 7:28)
- "Walk in the Spirit, and you shall not fulfill the lust of the flesh. For the flesh lusts against the Spirit, and the Spirit against the flesh: and these are contrary the one to the other." (Galatians 5:16-17)

And if any Christian finds himself or herself in an unhappy marriage, they just need to tough it out:

- "Every one who divorces his wife and marries another commits adultery, and he who marries a woman divorced from her husband commits adultery." (Luke 16:18) (RSV) See also Mark 10:11-12; Matthew 5:32; 19:9.

Of course, in heaven there will be no family relationships at all:

- "For when they shall rise from the dead, they neither marry nor are given in marriage, but are as the angels which are in heaven." (Mark 12:25) See also Luke 20:35-36 and Matthew 22:30.

And finally, some childrearing advice for Christian fathers who may have overlooked this one:

- "Fathers, provoke not your children to anger, lest they be discouraged." (Colossians 3:21)

No sinning after you're saved:

By the way some Christians live, you'd think that Christianity is just a license to behave badly, because you can always be forgiven in the end, as long as you repent before you die. But the Bible tells us that no backsliding is allowed. As we saw earlier, you only get one chance at forgiveness. So if you run into any Christians who have lapsed into any kind of sin after being saved, ask why they have not heeded these warnings, and say "See you in hell!"

- "If after they have escaped the pollutions of the world through the knowledge of the Lord and Saviour Jesus Christ, they are again entangled therein, and overcome, the latter end is worse with them than the beginning. For it had been better for them not to have known the way of righteousness, than, after they have known it, to turn from the holy commandment delivered unto them." (2 Peter 2:20-21)
- "For if we sin willfully after that we have received the knowledge of the truth, there remains no more sacrifice for sins, but a certain fearful looking for of judgment and fiery indignation." (Hebrews 10:26-27)
- "For it is impossible for those who were once enlightened, and have tasted of the heavenly gift, and were made partakers of the Holy Ghost, and have tasted the good word of God, and the powers of the world to come, if they shall fall away, to renew them again unto repentance; seeing they crucify to themselves the Son of

God afresh, and put him to an open shame." (Hebrews 6:4-6)

Immoral and Unjust Political Positions Supported by the New Testament:

Any Christian who bases his or her belief on the Bible has some heavy political baggage to carry around. As Western society has become more and more inclusive over the past few centuries, the New Testament view of political and social relations has remained stuck in a first century frame of mind. If you are a Bible-believing 21st century Christian, here are some of the political positions you subscribe to:

Subjection to political authorities:

In the New Testament, democracy is not an option. Freedom is not a value. Rulers are not responsive to the people. Rather, the people are the obedient subjects of the ruler. This is the divine right of kings, which we started chipping away at in 1215 with the signing of Magna Carta. But in the New Testament, it's preserved in all its primitive glory. The next time you hear a fundamentalist Christian complaining about taxes, or bureaucratic decisions in Washington, remind them that their Bible commands them to obey the government. For all political power is authorized by God - even when liberal Democrats are in charge.

- "Let every person be in subjection to the governing authorities. For there is no authority except from God, and those which exist are established by God.

Therefore, he who resists authority has opposed the ordinance of God." (Romans 13: 1-2) (RSV)

Note that this also applies to people living under the likes of Saddam Hussein, Stalin, and the Taliban. According to this view, even the plotters of June 20, 1944 were going against God's established authority when they contrived a plot to get rid of Hitler.

- "Submit yourselves to every ordinance of man for the Lord's sake: whether it be to the king, as supreme; or unto governors." (1 Peter 2:13-14)
- "For the same reason you also pay taxes, for the authorities are ministers of God, attending to this very thing. Pay all of them their dues, taxes to whom taxes are due, revenue to whom revenue is due, respect to whom respect is due, honor to whom honor is due." (Romans 13:6-7) (RSV)

Acceptance of slavery:

This hardly requires any comment, except to note that there are 111 occurrences in the NASB translation of the New Testament for the words "slave," "slaves," or "slavery." In addition, many instances of the word "servant" are actually the same Greek word (*doulos*) as those that are translated as "slave." The KJV often substitutes "servant" for "slave" (*doulos*) in its translation. However, this is misleading, because in Roman times there was no such thing as what we know as a "servant," that is, a free person who hires himself or herself out as domestic help or laborer, but is free to quit at any time. Such services were performed by slaves.

None of these biblical references to slavery even so much as hint at the possibility that there might be anything wrong with one human being owning another. In fact, the

Bible was often used to justify slavery in the American South before the Civil War.[3] Here's what true Christians have to believe if they accept the Bible as their authority:

- "Slaves, be obedient to those who are your masters according to the flesh, with fear and trembling, in the sincerity of your heart,as to Christ." (Ephesians 6:5) (NASB)
- "Slaves, in all things obey those who are your masters on earth." (Colossians 3:22) (NASB)
- "Bid slaves to be submissive to their masters and to give satisfaction in every respect." (Titus 2:9) (RSV)
- "All who are under the yoke as slaves are to regard their own masters as worthy of all honor so that the name of God and our doctrine will not be spoken against.
(1 Timothy 6:1-2) (NASB)

Women must be submissive:

Here is another area where modern society has improved upon first century beliefs. To be a true Christian, you have to believe that women are inferior to men, and are barred from any positions of leadership over men. (And no jewelry, either.)

- "Let your women keep silence in the churches: for it is not permitted unto them to speak; but they are commanded to be under obedience as also saith the law." (1 Corinthians 14:34)
- "Let a woman learn in silence with all submissiveness. I permit no woman to teach or to have authority over men; she is to keep silent." (1 Timothy 2:11-12) (RSV)
- "Wives, submit yourselves unto your own husbands, as unto the Lord. For the husband is the head of the wife,

---

[3] For example, Thornton Stringfellow, "A Scriptural View of Slavery," in *Slavery Defended* (Prentice-Hall, 1963), pp.86-98.

even as Christ is the head of the church." (Ephesians 5:22-23)
- "Neither was the man created for the woman, but the woman for the man." (1 Corinthians 11:9)
- Women should "adorn themselves in modest apparel, with shamefacedness and sobriety; not with braided hair, or gold, or pearls, or costly array." (1 Timothy 2:9)

Homosexuality is an unpardonable sin:

No ambiguity here. If you're a Bible-believing Christian, you think homosexuality is a sin, and an unforgiveable one at that. The Bible puts gay people into the same category as murderers and kidnappers:

- "Do not be deceived; neither the sexually immoral nor idolaters nor adulterers nor male prostitutes nor homosexual offenders nor thieves nor the greedy nor drunkards nor slanderers nor swindlers will inherit the kingdom of God." (1 Corinthians 6:9-10) (NIV)
- "For this reason God gave them over to degrading passions; for their women exchanged the natural function for that which is unnatural, and in the same way also the men abandoned the natural function of the woman and burned in their desire toward one another, men with men committing indecent acts and receiving in their own persons the due penalty of their error." (Romans 1:26-27) (NASB) There are Christians who consider AIDS to be the "due penalty" imposed by God for this "unnatural" behavior.
- "Law is not made for a righteous man, but for those who are lawless and rebellious, for the ungodly and sinners, for the unholy and profane, for those who kill their fathers or mothers, for murderers and immoral men and homosexuals and kidnappers and liars and perjurers, and whatever else is contrary to sound

teaching, according to the glorious gospel of the blessed God, with which I have been entrusted." (1 Timothy 1:9-11) (NASB)

Children of unbelievers are unclean:

To hear the fundamentalists tell it, all life is precious, even that of unborn children. However, if both parents of the child happen to be unbelievers, the poor child loses some of its preciousness. Ask your Christian opponents if abortion is okay as long as both parents are atheists.

- "For the unbelieving husband is sanctified by the wife, and the unbelieving wife is sanctified by the husband: else were your children unclean; but now are they holy." (1 Corinthians 7:14) (Implying that the children of two unbelievers would be unclean.)

The Bottom Line:

If Christians are going to be consistent with the teachings of their Bible, then they need to observe a standard of conduct that most of them don't even come close to meeting. By pointing out those passages that highlight the discrepancy, you can discredit their sincerity and cause them considerable discomfort as they try to explain their hypocrisy. Similarly, to be consistent with Biblical teachings, Christians must defend political positions on slavery, women, and homosexual rights that are considered primitive and unjust by most of us who live in the 21st century.

As we've seen in previous chapters, the logical inconsistency of Christianity as presented in the New Testament is already enough to discredit the Bible as the foundation of the Christian religion. The arguments of hypocrisy and political obsolescence are not aimed at the

Bible itself, but at its defenders. A Bible full of self-contradictions, plus a mass of hypocritical and politically authoritarian believers, adds up to a very difficult position to defend. For those who have not made up their minds yet, it's hard to see how this package would hold any attraction for them.

The Bottom Line

What have we learned from our examination of the New Testament? We have seen that the plain meaning of the words written by the New Testament authors leads to contradictions in details and doctrines, and that the only way to avoid these contradictions is to resort to highly implausible symbolic interpretations, invented facts, and specious historical arguments. What the apologists are really telling us is that the Bible does not mean what it says. They are telling us instead that the Bible means what *they* think it means, filtered through their own theological bias. This means that ordinary people cannot read the Bible and understand what it means, without being privy to these interpretive theories and imaginary facts which exist nowhere except in the fantasies of the apologists and theologians. If the Bible needs this much help from ordinary mortals in order to make sense, what is the likelihood that it is really the unerring inspired word of God?